HIGH GROUND WRECKS

3rd Edition

David J. Smith

Midland Counties Publications

Thanks

Printed in England by
BL&U Printing, Wellingborough and Arkle Print Limited, Northampton

Front and back cover photographs:
A 20 OTU Wellington in the Highlands. *(David J. Smith)*

Over the years many people have supplied valuable information and photographs which have been valuable in the compilation of this book. Among the major contributors have been Paul and Tom Allonby, Barry Blunt, Stephen Burns, Bill and Ian Carter, Victor Caruth, I. A. Clark, Ron Collier, Paul Connatty, Ernie Cromie, Geoff Cruikshank, Hywel Davies, Peter Dobson, Eddie Doylerush, J. Drake, Peter Durham, J. D. Earnshaw, Arthur Evans, Jim Ferguson, John Finch-Davies, Roger Freeman, Ken Haddleton, David Hanson, Philippa Hodgkiss, A. Robin Hood, John Huggon, Russell Ives, Philip Jones, S. Leslie, Andy Mackay, Alan Mark, John Martindale, John McDonald, Peter Moran, John Molyneux, C. D. Radford, Harold Roberts, Nick Roberts, Peter Rushden, Jim Rutland, Wallace Shackleton, Phillip Shaw, David Stansfield, Ed Stephenson, B. Stevens, Ray Sturtivant, David E. Thompson, A. C. Watson and Ralph Wood.

I do hope that anyone inadvertently omitted will forgive me; everyone's help, no matter how small, is appreciated, and will equally be so for future editions of this guide.

Photographs are by the author unless otherwise credited. We are sorry of some are not works of photographic art, but please remember that some are old, and all have been taken on rare visits to often inaccessible sites, and often not under the best of conditions.

HIGH GROUND WRECKS
David J. Smith

A 20 OTU Wellington in the Highlands.

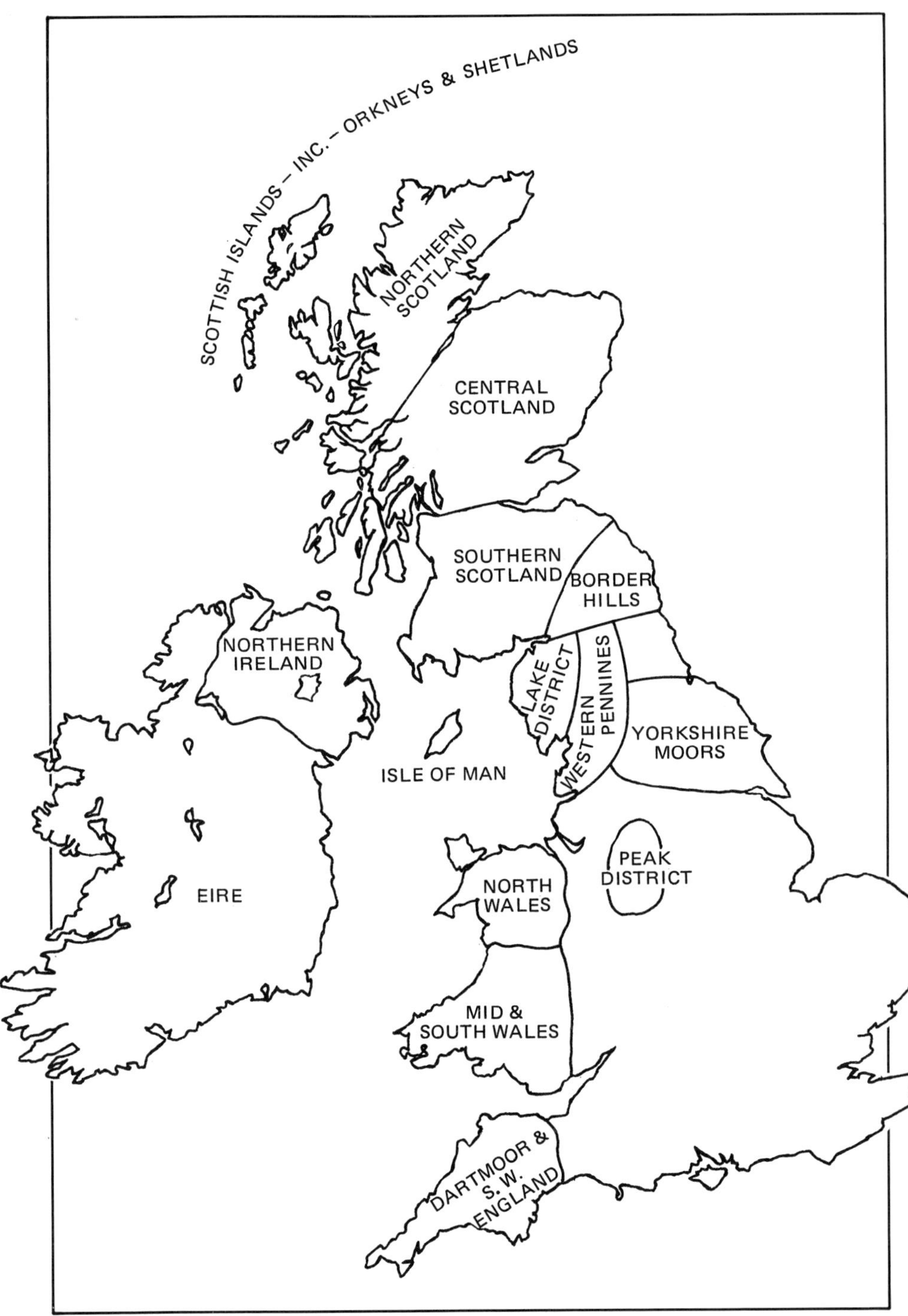

SCOTTISH ISLANDS - INC. - ORKNEYS & SHETLANDS
NORTHERN SCOTLAND
CENTRAL SCOTLAND
SOUTHERN SCOTLAND
BORDER HILLS
NORTHERN IRELAND
LAKE DISTRICT
WESTERN PENNINES
YORKSHIRE MOORS
ISLE OF MAN
EIRE
PEAK DISTRICT
NORTH WALES
MID & SOUTH WALES
DARTMOOR & S. W. ENGLAND

Contents

Introduction

The present work is the culmination of twenty-five years of research, not forgetting the expenditure of much sweat, foot-slogging and boot leather. I do not claim it to be definitive but know that it adds considerably to the information contained in the previous two editions published in 1976 and 1977 respectively and now out-of-print. A number of post-war crash sites have been included, some of the more recent ones hardly qualifying as historic but listed as they are sometimes confusingly close to wrecks of an earlier era.

My personal opinion is that the wreckage should be left undisturbed but unfortunately this view is not shared by everyone and a lot of pillaging has taken place. Recovering parts for museums is pardonable, but taking bits away to moulder in garden sheds and garages and eventually to be discarded is totally pointless. It should be remembered also that legally the wreckage of RAF and former enemy aircraft is Crown Property, and that Ministry of Defence permission is required for its removal. Responsibility for the remains of American aircraft has also been delegated to MoD.

Regrettably, in certain parts of the country - Snowdonia and the Lake District are two examples - the National Park Authorities have seen fit to organise the removal of much of the surviving wreckage. The aim, no doubt, is to eliminate an 'eyesore' but, since the pieces are all but invisible from more than a hundred yards away it seems to me to be an over-reaction. There are far worse excesses in the National Parks and I believe that these fragments on hillsides should be acknowledged as a form of memorial to the airmen who so often died in the accidents. Objectors should reflect that this tragic loss of life was part of a struggle to retain our freedom, one of whose privileges is to walk the hills.

Finally, a word of warning; the potential hazards of hill-walking are many. Beginners are urged to consult one of the numerous outdoor guides for information and advice on essential equipment and tactics. That said, there are many other aesthetic pleasures to be found in the mountains apart from looking at the remains of old aeroplanes. Some of the wildest and most beautiful country in the British Isles is to be savoured. I hope that readers will derive as much enjoyment from this blend of climbing, walking and aviation history as the writer.

David J. Smith
Bebington, Merseyside
December 1988

Notes on Using This Book

This book is basically organised as a series of commentaries and listings of High Ground Wrecks in sections covering the British Isles roughly from north to south. The boundaries are somewhat arbitrary and, except for the addition of a new area, the Isle of Man, remain unchanged from the previous editions. The unwieldy 'landscape' format of the previous editions has however been replaced by a conventional size made possible by sub-dividing the lists under aircraft type with entries listed chronologically under each type. I trust that these changes will make for ease of reference for those seeking to locate particular information quickly.

The map references quoted refer to the Ordnance Survey 1:50 000 Metric Map, the sheet number or, in the case of the separate Northern Ireland series, the grid letter, appearing before the six figure map reference. A simple explanation of how to plot these grid references appears in the margin of each map and the reader is reminded that the pre-metric one inch to the mile maps, dating back to the 'fifties, conform to the same grid, although the sheet numbers are different.

Where the exact position of a crash site is not known, the north and south grid lines nearest to the officially recorded location are given, for example 109/ 66-15-. Occasionally, I have not been able to trace the geographical name, although it may appear on larger scale OS maps. In these cases, a question mark has been inserted after the appropriate sheet number.

The locations given in official records are often vague or mis-spelt, particularly where Welsh and Gaelic names are involved! Sometimes, a bearing and distance from a particular point are given or a latitude and longitude or a reference from an obsolete wartime map grid. The Operations Record Books of the unit to which the aircraft belonged and those of the various organisations handling or reporting the crash often give widely-differing positions for the site. For example, according to their respective unit ORBs and the Accident Record Cards held at the MoD's Air Historical Branch, Wellingtons DV800 and HE466 both crashed on Snowdon. The actual positions are in the Carnedd Range, anything up to ten miles from Snowdon itself, which serves to illustrate how nebulous the supposedly authoritative sources can be.

To avoid tedious repetition, I have devised a formula to describe the extent of remaining wreckage, as last recorded.

S Small pieces
M Medium remains, e.g. engine(s), undercarriage, fairly large pieces of airframe.
L Large remains - alas, a rare category — where the aircraft, or at least large sections of it are reasonably intact.
X Not known, i.e. not visited by me or friends and correspondents.

Serial numbers with quotation marks indicate mistakes in the official records which I have not yet been able to correct. Not previously included are the names of the airfields from which the aircraft were operating and their destinations. When only one airfield is shown, it may be assumed that the subject was on a cross-country navigational exercise (Navex). returning to its point of departure. Where training units possessed a satellite aerodrome, it is not always possible to determine from the ORB whether the aircraft had taken off from this or the parent station. Thus, particularly where bomber OTUs are concerned, there may be the occasional anomaly.

Many of the airfields in the lists are long disused, but there are a number of guides to their history and location, Patrick Stephens' 'Action Stations' series being the best known. For those readers who may not be familiar with the complicated system of RAF training and support units during the Second World War, a brief summary is as follows:

Elementary Flying Training Schools - basic pilot training, usually on Tiger Moths or Magisters.

(Pilot) Advanced Flying Units - twin-conversion on Oxfords for future bomber and coastal pilots, Masters or Harvards for fighter pilots.

Operational Training Units - intensive practice in operational flying techniques and, at the same time, conversion onto heavier types of aircraft. In the case of fighter pilots, conversion onto high performance aircraft such as the Spitfire, Hurricane and Typhoon.

(Heavy) Conversion Units - for four-engined bomber crews immediately prior to joining a squadron.

Air Observer Navigation Schools, Air Observers Schools and **(Observer) Advanced Flying Units** turned out navigators, or observers as they were originally called, and bomb aimers. The designation of these schools changed as the war progressed. There were many other less important units whose names adequately describe their tasks.

The Air Transport Auxiliary was a civilian organisation whose men and women ferried aircraft for the RAF. Their regulations forbade cloud flying but, such was the importance of the job, many perished in bad weather crashes when delivering aircraft to the squadrons from Maintenance Units or the manufacturers.

Chapter One

Northern Scotland

For the purposes of this book, I have defined this region as the landmass north of a line running east-west roughly through Inverness. It includes the North-West Highlands, the largest wilderness in Britain and the remote mountains and moors of Sutherland. It must be emphasised that wreck-hunting trips in this area must be planned with extreme care, and proper equipment is essential. There are surprisingly large tracts of country in which no wrecks are reported and one wonders if there any which remain undiscovered. Certainly, if any missing aircraft still exist in Britain this is where they are likely to be found. A promising rumour involved a Focke-Wulf Condor on Mullach Coire Mhic Fhearchair in Wester Ross, but this is now known to be false. Another favourite story concerns the Sopwith Camel allegedly found during the search for the Anson on Ben More Assynt. Again, it seems to have no foundation.

The terrain in the North was highly unsuitable for airfields, the handful established during the war meeting the minimum strategic requirements. They were the Coastal Command station at Wick and its nearby satellite at Skitten, a fighter base at Castletown, near Thurso, for their protection and also that of the Fleet Anchorage at Scapa Flow. Farther south, there was a small clutch of aerodromes along the Cromarty Firth, consisting of Tain, a large Coastal Command base, Evanton, an air gunnery school later taken over by the Fleet Air Arm, and Fearn, another Royal Naval Air Station used for training. RAF Alness, formerly Invergordon, was an important flying boat base, relegated later in the war to Sunderland and Catalina operational training.

Today's Inverness Airport at Dalcross was used at various times as an air gunners' school and for advanced pilot training. To the east lie the important airfields of Kinloss and Lossiemouth. They are still very much a part of the front-line RAF but in the Second World War they had a training role. Kinloss was a night bomber Operational Training Unit, No.19, equipped with Whitleys, while No.20 OTU was performing the same task at Lossiemouth with Wellingtons. Many of the aircraft were tired veterans withdrawn from the squadrons and the combination of treacherous weather, rugged mountains and inexperience proved fatal for many of the pupil crews on cross-country navigational exercises.

A particularly interesting site can be found near Berriedale, where the Sunderland carrying the Duke of Kent and his entourage to Iceland crashed. The circumstances have long remained a mystery and a full account, together with possible answers, can be found in my article in *After the Battle* magazine no.37. The salvage team was given special orders to clear the wreckage completely, but a few fragments remain close to the Celtic Cross which commemorates the incident.

Whitley P5005 on Burgie Hill is the famous DY-N on which, during its earlier service with No.102 Squadron, the then Pilot Officer Leonard Cheshire gained the DSO. He flew the bomber back from Cologne with an enormous hole in the fuselage after flak ignited the flares. Another Whitley, this time in Glen Carron, was returning to Yorkshire from a raid over Germany but such was the dearth of navigational aids during the early years of the war that the crew became completely lost and perished in the enusing crash.

On the opposite side of the glen, a Marauder crew were killed when they apparently descended too soon on a ferry flight to Prestwick via Iceland. Another disaster befell the fifteen occupants of a Liberator near Gairloch, all the more tragic because they were on their way home. A memorial plaque has been placed at the site recently. I have included a further American aircraft, the US Navy Vindicator, for interest only. Having visited it a few years ago, I can confirm that only scraps of metal and blue-painted fabric are left.

The crew of the Anson on Ben More Assynt were the only airmen buried on high ground in Britain, the cairn of stones marking the grave having been renovated in 1985. The crash happened in the days before a proper mountain rescue service existed and it became policy thereafter to recover bodies no matter how difficult or unpleasant this might be. The Commonwealth War Graves Commission have placed a memorial beside the gateway to Inchnadamph Church listing the names of the crew.

Below: **The engine and propeller remains from the 19 OTU Anson N9857, which crashed on Ben More Assynt.**

Opposite: **Fin of 818 Sqn Barracuda PM870 on Col Bheinn, lost while on a training flight from Fearn.**

AIRSPEED OXFORD

| 17.04.40 | N4735 | 14 SFTS | Cairn Uish. Kinloss. *29/187503* | S |
| 06.12.51 | V3910/76 | 8 AFTS | Findhorn. Local flying from Dalcross. *27/903411* | S |

ARMSTRONG WHITWORTH WHITLEY

24.09.40	P5006	19 OTU	Ben Aigan. Navex from Kinloss, dived out of cloud. *27/31-48-*	X
27.02.41	P4996	78 Sqn	Glen Carron. Lost returning to Dishforth from ops. *25/?*	S
01.05.41	P5070	612 Sqn	Scaraben. Anti-sub patrol from Wick. *17/083276*	S
15.06.42	P5005	19 OTU	Burgie Hill. Turning error on controlled descent through cloud to Kinloss. *27/10-55-*	X
12-13.3.42	BD678/ WL-R	612 Sqn	Ben Hutig. On convoy escort from Wick. *10/543665*	S
17.05.43	BD295/M	19 OTU	Cawdor Moor. Navex from Kinloss. *27/811409*	S
28.08.43	Z9469	19 OTU	4 miles south of Kinloss. Navex from Kinloss. *27/?*	X

AVRO ANSON

13.04.41	N9857	19 OTU	Ben More Assynt. Cross-country from Kinloss. Wreck found by shepherd 26.05.41. *15/294232*	L
18.08.42	DJ178/G	20 OTU	East Scaraben. Descended too soon on last leg of cross-country navex from Lossiemouth. *17/089282*	S
24.04.44	AX435/S	19 OTU	Carn Na Cailliche. Hit hill in downdraught. All crew survived. Kinloss. *27/19-47-*	X

AVRO LANCASTER

| 14.03.51 | TX264/ BS-D | 120 Sqn | Beinn Eighe. Night navex from Kinloss. *19/943601* | L |

CONSOLIDATED B-24 LIBERATOR

| 18.04.44 | BZ724/P | 59 Sqn | Near Helmsdale. Diverting to Tain after anti-sub patrol from Ballykelly. Captain was sole survivor. *17/975152* | X |
| 13.06.45 | 42-95095 | 44th BG | Near Gairloch. Prestwick/Iceland. *19/84-76-* | M |

DE HAVILLAND MOSQUITO

| 05.04.43 | DZ486 | 618 Sqn | Ben Spionnaidh. Bombing exercise from Skitten. *9/36-57-* | M |

ENGLISH ELECTRIC CANBERRA

| 02.02.66 | WT531 | 80 Sqn | Sron Garbh. Bruggen/Lossiemouth. *17/058261* | L |

FAIREY BARRACUDA

| 15-16.12.44 | MX691 | 814 Sqn | 6 miles north-west of Berriedale. Night navex from Fearn. *17/037293* | S |
| 14.07.45 | PM870 | 818 Sqn | Col Bheinn. Fearn. *17/886104* | |

FAIREY FULMAR ?

| - | - | | Near Westerdale. Crater and small pieces with Fairey Inspection stamps. Two crew baled out. *11/177503* | S |

HANDLEY PAGE HAMPDEN

| 25.08.43 | P2118/ Z9-D | 519 Sqn | Ben Loyal. Returning to Wick from search for a missing Hampden. *10/583498* | M |

HAWKER SEA HAWK

| 04.09.57 | WV845 | AWTF | Near Brora. Lossiemouth. *17/889080* | X |
| 05.05.59 | WM986/ 616-LM | 736 Sqn | Findhorn. Lossiemouth. *27/893336* | S |

MARTIN B-26 MARAUDER

| 03.06.43 | 41-34707 | 455 BS/ 322 BG | Beinn Na Feusaige. Ferrying Meeks Field (Iceland)/ Prestwick. *25/088543* | S |

SHORT SUNDERLAND

| 25.08.42 | W4026/M | 228 Sqn | Near Dunbeath. Invergordon/Iceland. 14 killed including HRH Duke of Kent. Rear gunner survived. Memorial at site. | |
| 15.08.44 | DP197 | 4 OTU | Creag Riabhach. Recalled to base at Alness due to weather deterioration. 15 killed | X |

VICKERS WELLINGTON

30.07.41	R1093	20 OTU	Carn Garbh. Navex from Lossiemouth. *17/895139*	M
05.12.41	L4348	20 OTU	Near Tongue. Navex from Lossiemouth. *10/759457*	M
14.02.42	N2825	20 OTU	Near Rothes. Navex from Lossiemouth. *28/?*	M
14.11.43	HF746	20 OTU	Ben Rinnes. Navex from Lossiemouth. *27/257358*	S

VOUGHT SIKORSKY VINDICATOR

| 23.04.42 | 1363 | VS-71 | Allt on Tor. Cleared early 1970s, only tiny pieces remain. Flying Tain/Longman from USS *Wasp* in Scapa Flow. *21/636773* | |

Opposite: **The sturdy structure of the Barracuda is evident in the remains of PM870.**
Above: **Liberator 42-95095 was returning to the USA when it crashed near Gairloch.**
Below: **The few remains of Marauder 41-34707 in Glen Carron.**

Chapter Two

Scottish Islands

Aircraft remains on the islands represent a fair cross-section of wartime types. Strictly speaking, not all were as a result of collisions with high ground but have been included for interest. Salvage was not always possible for reasons of inaccessibility so wrecks were often broken up and buried where they had fallen. For example, bad weather and a four mile climb delayed the salvage of the Dakota on Mull and the majority of the aircraft was eventually dumped in a nearby ravine to render it invisible to overflying aircraft and thus avoid any further crash reports which would have to be investigated.

The Hebrides, Orkney and Shetland support a number of aerodromes, many of them built on far from ideal terrain at great expense in labour and materials and often dangerously close to high ground. They were, however, strategically essential to support Coastal Command operations, Transatlantic ferrying and fighter cover for Scapa Flow, Loch Ewe and other naval bases. One of the few lasting social benefits of the war was a chain of airfields, more than adequate for postwar communications with the mainland.

Stornoway became an important staging post for short range aircraft ferrying through Iceland to Prestwick, its American-operated radio beacon serving also as a navigational aid for those overflying. Benbecula and Tiree were both used by Coastal Command for convoy escort duties and Port Ellen on Islay supported a Ferry Training Unit specialising in the Beaufighter, two being lost on the nearby hills. Sumburgh was another coastal base, and flying boat squadrons flew from Sullom Voe in the north of Shetland. Orkney had four aerodromes, two of them for naval training at Hatston and Twatt, the others being fighter stations at Skeabrae and Kirkwall.

Few enthusiasts seem to have visited the Orkney wrecks, hence their present condition and exact location is uncertain. The Liberator on Hoy was not salvaged but its remains were dragged to the foot of the mountain and buried by the salvage team. On the Isle of Skye, the same was done with the B-17 which had hit Ben Edra, but much of it still lies in the rocky gullies.

I am told that the tail and engines from the Heinkel 111 which crash-landed on Fair Isle were removed in recent years when an airstrip was built, but may still be in the vicinity. On Foula, large sections of the Canadian Canso amphibian were scattered across the small island by gales and much of it has now been cleared. The same fate befell the Oxford on Auskerry. Although it landed intact, it was totally demolished by a storm within days but parts may survive on the island.

On one of the most remote and forbidding island groups, that of St Kilda, are the remains of three aircraft. By coincidence they were all from Ferry Training Units which often used the islands as a turning point on navigational exercises. One of them is an unidentified Wellington which is almost certainly LA995 of No.303 FTU, Stornoway which failed to return to base on 23 February 1943. A comprehensive account of this and the other St Kilda accidents can be found in *After the Battle* magazine number 30.

The most southerly of the major Scottish islands is Arran, its jagged mountains ideally placed to trap unwary crews flying from Prestwick and other aerodromes in South-West Scotland. On Beinn Nuis the remains of three American aircraft lie within half a mile of one another, parts of the B-17 still embedded in the cliff face where it impacted. The US Navy Liberator almost made it to Prestwick from the USA but failed to clear the Beinn Nuis ridge by only a few feet. The identity of a nearby Lodestar is a mystery but it probably belonged to the 1403rd Base Unit at Prestwick and was perhaps on a liaison flight to Stornoway.

Another Arran wreck was Liberator AM261 of the Atlantic Ferry Organisation. It had taken off from RAF Ayr for Gander and, despite a very experienced crew, failed to clear Am Binein, the adjacent mountain to the better-known Goat Fell. All twenty-one on board, many of them American and Canadian ferry crews, were killed and are buried at Lamlash. An Anson crashed close to the Liberator the same year, but only small panels, some with trainer yellow paint, can be found.

The islands tend to resemble giant sponges and walking any great distance soon becomes tiring, particularly as paths are scarce. Some of the mountain ranges, on Skye, Jura and Arran to name but a few, are extremely rugged and expeditions should be planned accordingly.

Outer wing section of Chesapeake AL941 on Arran.

AVRO ANSON

28.01.41	N4939	1 AONS	Am Binein, Arran. Navex from Prestwick. *69/00-42-*		S
02.08.42	DJ472	1 OAFU	Caisteal Abhail, Arran. Navex from Wigtown. *69/99-42-*		S

BOEING B-17G FORTRESS

10.12.45	42-97186	388th BG	Beinn Nuis, Arran. Knettishall/Prestwick. *69/957398*		M
03.03.45	44-83325	Unassigned	Beinn Edra, Skye. Ferrying Meeks Field/Valley. *23/456630*		M

BRISTOL BEAUFIGHTER

03.06.43	LX798	304 FTU	Conachair, St Kilda. Navex from Port Ellen. *18/099003*		S
12.09.43	LX946	304 FTU	Near Port Ellen. In circuit area. *60/?*		S
12.09.43	LZ146	304 FTU	Near Port Ellen. In circuit area. *60/?*		S

BRISTOL BEAUFORT

30.08.42	L4479	5 OTU	Goat Fell, Arran. Navex from Turnberry. *69/987408*	S
03.09.42	L9803/Y	TTU	Ben More, Mull. Navex from Abbotsinch. *48/523334*	M

BRISTOL BLENHEIM

03.09.41	L9261	235 Sqn	Huxter Walls, Shetland. Sumburgh. *3/19-56-*	X

CHANCE VOUGHT CORSAIR

11.07.44	JT461/7C	1841 Sqn	Hoy, Orkney. Hatston/HMS *Formidable. 7/?*	X

CONSOLIDATED CATALINA

15.07.41	AH533	210 Sqn	Jura. Patrol from Oban. *61/?*	X
19.01.42	Z2151	240 Sqn	Yell, Shetland. Circling at night waiting for flarepath to be changed. Castle Archdale/Sullom Voe. *1/?*	M
12.05.44	JX273	302 FTU	Vatersay. Navex from Oban. *31/641957*	L

CONSOLIDATED CANSO

29.7.44	11062	162 Sqn	Foula. Anti-sub patrol from Wick. *4/948396*	M

CONSOLIDATED LIBERATOR

10.08.41	AM261	ATFERO	Am Binein, Arran. Ayr/Gander. 21 killed. *69/004425*	S
20.08.43	42-41030	Knox Prov Group	Beinn Nuis, Arran. US Navy PBY4-1. Ferrying Iceland/Prestwick. *69/957396*	L
15.09.43	42-72851	USAAF	North Lee, North Uist. Ferrying Iceland/Prestwick. *18/93-66-.*	M
01.01.45	FL949/Y	311 Sqn	Hoy. Mostly buried by MU. Patrol from Tain. *7/208030*	A

DOUGLAS DAKOTA

01.02.45	KK194	45 Gp	Ben Talaidh, Mull. Ferrying Iceland/Prestwick. *48/62-35-.*	L

FAIREY BARRACUDA

?.01.45	LS931		Paps of Jura. *61/497737*	M

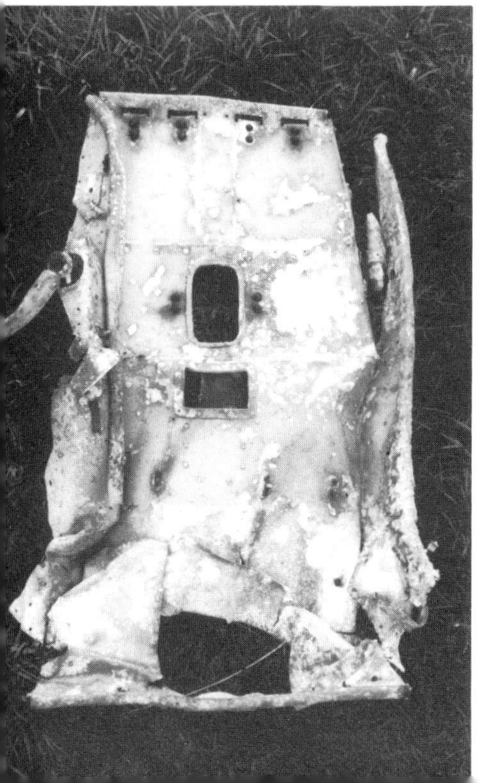

A selection of photographs depicting the crash site of Beaufort L9803 on Ben More. *Opposite:* the identity visible on a starboard engine panel; *above:* view of collected wreckage includes *below left* pilot's seat, *below right* oil tank remains *(all M. Elliott)*

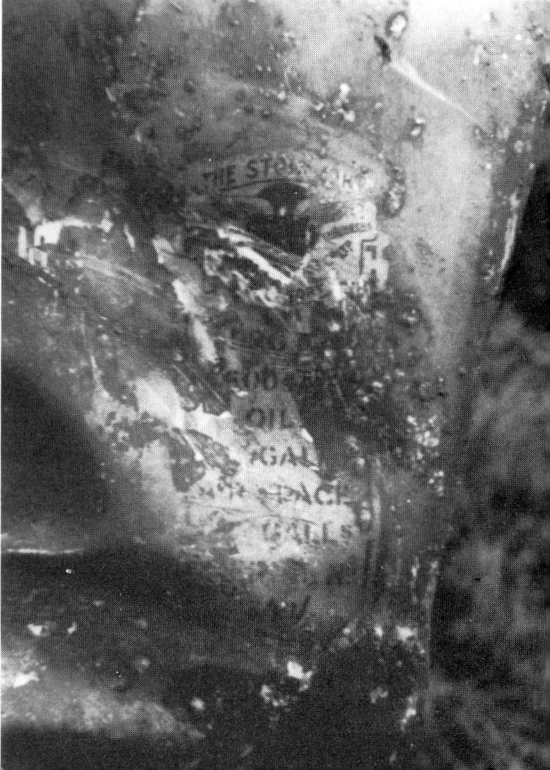

FAIREY FIREFLY
25.09.51   WB336   719 Sqn Islay. Training flight from Eglinton. *60/?*   L

GENERAL DYNAMICS F-111F
07.12.82   70-2377   48 TFW Na Stri, Skye. Lakenheath. *32/50-19-*   X

GRUMMAN MARTLET
04.06.43   FN248   878 Sqn Orkney. Night training flight from Hatston.   X
04.06.43   FN288   878 Sqn Orkney. Night training flight from Hatston.   X

HANDLEY PAGE HALIFAX
09.04.45   JP165/D   58 Sqn Harris. Met sortie from Stornoway. *14/?*   M

HAWKER HUNTER
12.02.80   XK151/Z   2 TWU Bla Bheinn, Skye. *32/53-22-*   X

HAWKER HURRICANE
06.02.44   LF207   516 Sqn Coll. On combined operations exercise from Connel. *46/?* S

HEINKEL He 111
17.01.41   2645/   Wekusta Fair Isle. Tail and engines believed removed when new airstrip
           T5+EU   Od.d.L. built. Probably from Stavanger. *4/212717*

LOCKHEED HUDSON
19.03.41   N7310   220 Sqn Red Hill of Sneuk, Hoy. On patrol from Wick. *6/24-21-*   X
31.07.42   FH375/W 500 Sqn Lewis. Air test from Stornoway. *8/?*   L

LOCKHEED C-60 LODESTAR
?.12.43   1403rd BU? Beinn Nuis, Arran. Prestwick? *69/956401*   S

SHORT SUNDERLAND
08.06.44   ML858   302 FTU St Kilda. Navex from Oban. *18/096998*   X

SUPERMARINE SEAFIRE
19.06.43   886 Sqn Auchdreoch, Arran. Machrihanish. Area now afforested.
                                 69/99-24-   X

SUPERMARINE SPITFIRE
23.09.41   X4108   124 Sqn Rendall, Orkney. Convoy escort from Castletown. *6/?*   X
19.06.43   R7198   8 OTU Skye. Cross-country from Dyce. *23 or 33/?*   X

VICKERS WELLINGTON
23.02.43? LA995? 303 FTU? Soay, St Kilda. Almost definitely LA995 lost in this area on
                              navex from Stornoway.   M

VOUGHT SIKORSKY CHESAPEAKE
22.07.43   AL941   772 Sqn Glen Catacol, Arran. Exercise from Machrihanish. *69/93-46-* M

Opposite: **Views of the wreckage of Dakota KK194 buried in a gully by the salvage crew close to the crash site on the Isle of Mull, include part of the fin** (*lower left*).
Top right: **A citation in Salen church awarded to the people of Salen and Glen Forsa for their rescue attempts of the crew of KK194 on Ben Talaidh** (*all Max Elliott*)

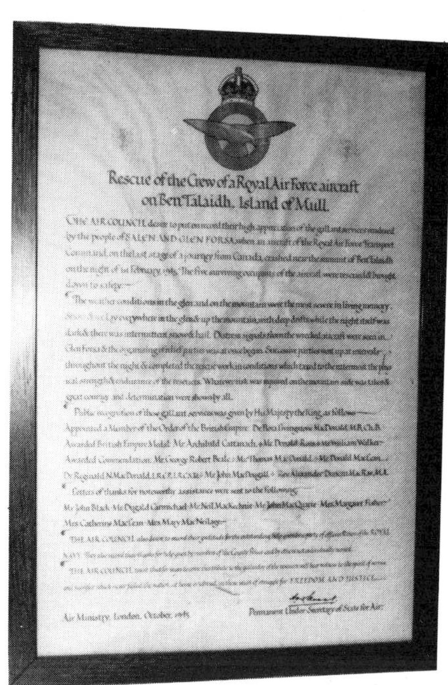

Rescue of the Crew of a Royal Air Force aircraft on Ben Talaidh, Island of Mull.

THE AIR COUNCIL desire to put on record their high appreciation of the gallant services rendered by the people of SALEN AND GLEN FORSA when an aircraft of the Royal Air Force Transport Command, on the last stage of a journey from Canada, crashed near the summit of Ben Talaidh on the night of 1st February 1945. The five surviving occupants of the aircraft were rescued & brought down to safety—

The weather conditions in the glen and on the mountain were the most severe in living memory, snow lying deep everywhere in the glen & up the mountain, with deep drifts, while the night itself was dark & there was intermittent snow & hail. Distress signals from the wrecked aircraft were seen in Glen Forsa & the organising of relief parties was at once begun. Successive parties went up & carried on throughout the night & completed the rescue work in conditions which taxed to the utmost the physical strength & endurance of the rescuers. Whatever risk was required on the mountain side was taken & great courage and determination were shown by all.

Public recognition of these gallant services was given by His Majesty the King as follows:—

Appointed a Member of the Order of the British Empire: Dr Flora Livingstone MacDonald, M.B., Ch.B.

Awarded British Empire Medal: Mr Archibald Cattanach, & Mr Donald Rankin, & William Walker.

Awarded Commendation: Mr George Robert Beale, & Mr Thomas MacDonald, & Mr Donald MacGillivray, & Dr Reginald N. MacDonald, L.R.C.P.I. R.C.S.Ed., & Mr John MacDougall, & Rev Alexander Duncan, M.A., B.D., M.A.

Letters of thanks for noteworthy assistance were sent to the following:—

Mr John Black, Mr Dugald Carmichael, Mr Neil MacLachlan, Mr John MacQuarie, Mrs Margaret Fisher, Mrs Catherine MacLean, Miss Mary MacNeilage.—

THE AIR COUNCIL also desire to record their gratitude for the outstanding help given by parties of officers & men of the ROYAL NAVY. They also record their thanks for help given by members of the Coastal Forces and to those not individually named.

THE AIR COUNCIL trust that the many acts of heroism which took place in the glen & on the mountain will have a value to the people of every succeeding age which cannot be measured, & have endured, & shown, such of strength for FREEDOM AND JUSTICE.

Air Ministry, London, October 1945.

Permanent Under Secretary of State for Air

Chapter Three

Central Scotland

Taking a line through the Firths of Forth and Clyde as its southern extremity, this region encompasses the Cairngorms, Grampians, Trossachs and several lesser known ranges. The largest number of wrecks is to be found on the Grampians in the vicinity of Glen Clova, Glen Esk and Glen Isla. Further to the north-west are the Cairngorms which contain relatively few crash sites. Despite their inaccessibility, the aircraft are very broken up and rather disappointing. Only the very experienced should venture into this rugged country and some of the wrecks ideally require a two-day expedition.

The Wellingtons and Whitleys from Lossiemouth and Kinloss are scattered throughout the Highlands and the training aerodrome at Montrose saw many Masters and Oxfords take off never to return. Two of the aircraft lost in the mountains seem to have been missing for the longest period of any high ground crash in Britain, apart from the Spitfire on the Brecon Beacons (*qv*). One was Oxford PH404 found by climbers seven months after it vanished, the other was a Master from Montrose, AZ333, missing for nearly eight months and also discovered by chance.

No further information has come to light to confirm or deny the legend of the Sopwith Camel wreck in the Grampians. The Albemarle near Kenmore was probably on low ground and was being flown by a Russian crew who were training on the type before delivering a batch of them to the USSR. The Voodoo on Maol Odhar was missing for more than a week, during which an intensive air search was mounted using Prestwick as a base. The unprecented efforts gave rise to speculation that it was carrying something sensitive, but nothing was ever admitted publicly.

The rarely visited Monadhliath Mountains contain the remains of a Lancaster which disintegrated in mid-air, spreading wreckage over several miles. Another Lancaster broke up near Loch Lomond, some pieces falling to earth on Conic Hill. The same fate appears to have befallen the Halifax in Glen Isla.

The Youth Hostel in Glen Affric probably still uses parts of a crashed Wellington for various domestic functions. The aircraft plunged into the glen after the crew baled out during a night exercise. They were unable to maintain height after one engine failed over the mountains and a forced-landing attempt would have been suicidal. A Wellington from the same unit flew into Ben Alder at a position so far from a road that salvage would appear to have been impossible. However, to the annoyance of a later generation of aviation archaeologists, an Indian Army unit training in the area removed it piecemeal with pack mules!

The Mosquito in Glen Esk was flying the celebrated Stockholm courier service when it disappeared while returning to Leuchars after an engine failure. A month later the wreckage was found by a game-keeper. The stream at the head of which it had crashed is known locally as the 'Mosquito Burn' and perhaps this name will one day find its way onto the OS Map. Another aircraft of some historical importance crashed in the Ochil Hills above Alloa in 1941. It was Liberator AM926 which had taken part in several recent actions against U-boats. The fighter OTU at Grangemouth lost three Spitfires in the Ochils but no trace of either these or the Liberators have yet been found.

The burned-out remains of the B-29 near Lochgoilhead are a sad and sobering sight. All twenty on board were killed and the largest parts of the wreck are an outer wing, the tail turret, two engines and the massive undercarriage forgings. A few miles away can be found the quite large pieces of an early Grumman Martlet.

The Whitley which crashed near Balquhidder in November 1940 was once one of Scotland's most interesting wrecks. When I went to it in 1968 it was all there apart from the burned-out front fuselage. Since then it has been progressively pillaged, both privately and by service personnel. A propeller was set up at the Forest Centre at Strathyre as a memorial to the crew, but I am not sure if it is still there. The rear gunner was the sole survivor and local legend has it that he hid for several days believing that he was in enemy territory. This tale is told about other crash survivors, however!

AIRSPEED OXFORD

31.01.40	N6320	15 SFTS	Glen Buchat. Navex from Lossiemouth. *37/?*	X
02.03.42	L4597	45 MU	Loch Laidon. Engines now recovered. Ferrying Cambridge/ Kinloss. *41/390545*	S
03.09.42	N6438	2 FIS	Meluncart. Montrose. *43/629819*	S
12.10.43	HM724	19 PAFU	Cairngorms. Sucked onto mountain top by downdraught. Crew unhurt but had a long walk! Dalcross	S
26.10.44	DF448	2 FIS	Shank of Donald Young. Navex from Montrose. *44/42-74-*	X
10.01.45	PH404	311 Sqn	Bheinn A'Buird. Somewhere in England/Tain. Wreck found by climbers	M
24.08.50	PH311	66 Gp CF	Cairn Trench. Turnhouse/Dyce. *44/391736*	S

ARMSTRONG WHITWORTH ALBEMARLE

29.05.43	P1503	305 FTU	Near Kenmore. Probably cleared. On navex from Errol. Russian crew killed. *52/?*	X

ARMSTRONG WHITWORTH WHITLEY

24.11.40	P5090/L	502 Sqn	Fathan Glinne. Lost returning to Aldergrove from anti-sub patrol. *57/474169*	M
23-24.3.42	Z6933/Z	19 OTU	Finalty Hill. Kinloss. Wreck found 05.06.42. *44/218765*	M
31.01.43	LA837/F	19 OTU	Cromdale Hills. On navex from Kinloss. *36/140295*	X
03.07.43	LA877/W	19 OTU	Meallan Odhar. Engine failure on night bombing practice from Kinloss. *36/527806*	S
26.05.44	EB384/U	19 OTU	Glen Esk. One wing almost intact. Navex from Kinloss. *44/324808*	M

AVRO ANSON

07.08.41	R9584	20 OTU	Glen Avon. Seen to dive into hill, possibility of sabotage to elevator controls. 8 killed. Elgin/Turnhouse. *36/?*	X
21.08.42	DJ106	19 OTU	Ben McDhui. Navex from Kinloss. Memorial on site	M

AVRO LANCASTER

31.08.44	'PD259'/ JO-G	463 Sqn	Monadhliath Mts. Mid-air break up whilst returning to Waddington fron ops. *35/?*	S
13.09.44	PB456	101 Sqn	Conic Hill. Mid-air break up on navex from Ludford Magna. *56/420932*	S

AVRO VULCAN

12.06.63	XH477	44 Sqn	Hill of St Colm. Training flight from Finningley. *44/493884*	S

BAe JAGUAR

23.11.79	XX762/28	226 OCU	Beinn A'Chleibh. Lossiemouth. *50/25-27-*	X

BOEING B-29 SUPERFORTRESS

17.01.49	44-62276	301st BG	Succoth Glen. 20 killed. Scampton/Keflavik. *56/161022*	L

Above: A substantial amount of wreckage of Whitley P5090 on Fathan Glinne, included an engine and, *opposite,* a whole wing, most of which has now gone.

BRISTOL BEAUFIGHTER
03.03.43   EL335/P   235 Sqn   Six miles north west of Edzell. Leuchars. *44/?*   X

BRISTOL BEAUFORT
08.03.42   AW242   217 Sqn   Wirren. Leuchars/Wick. *44/513740*   M

BRISTOL BLENHEIM
06.04.41   L1500   141 Sqn   Gargunnock Hills. Crash-landing. Crew survived. Ayr. *57/69-92-*   X
10.12.41   ?/P   254 Sqn   Glen Isla. Aldergrove/Dyce. *44/?*   X
26.03.45   Z7356   526 Sqn   Cairngorms. Descended too soon to break cloud. Digby/Longman   M

CESSNA 150
17.11.81   G-BFHL   Ben Ledi. Inverness/Glasgow. *57/56-10-*   X

CONSOLIDATED LIBERATOR
10.12.41   AM926/ OH-F   120 Sqn   Tarmangie Hill. This aircraft had made the squadron's first attack on a U-boat on 22.10.41. Dyce/Nutts Corner. *58/94-01-*   X
17.10.44   KG857   547 Sqn   Wirren. On anti-sub patrol. Captain and three others survived. Leuchars. *44/521735*   M

DE HAVILLAND MOSQUITO
17.08.43   G-AGGF   BOAC   Glen Esk. Returning due to malfunction. Found by gamekeeper 08.09.43. Leuchars/Stockholm. *44/351806*   M

DE HAVILLAND TIGER MOTH
30.10.42   ?   11 EFTS   Near Kippen. Crew walked 4½ miles to safety. Perth. *57/?*   X
17.10.44   T5466   11 EFTS   3 miles north-west of Fettercairn. Perth. *45/?*   X
29.08.57   G-AKCH   Blainenon. Engine only. Perth/Donibristle. *58/863019*

ENGLISH ELECTRIC CANBERRA
22.11.56   WJ615   50 Sqn   Carn An t'Sagairt Mor. Kinloss/Upwood. *44/206845*   L

FAIREY ALBACORE

01.05.41	?	767 Sqn?	Glen Clova. Arbroath. *44/277784*	M
31.05.43	L7138	9 PAFU	5 miles north of Clova Inn. Forced-landing, presumed recovered. Errol. *44/?*	

FAIREY FIREFLY

16.05.49	Z2108/ 245-LM	766 Sqn	Lochnagar. Yellow painted wreckage visible from a distance. Lossiemouth. *44/263848*	L

FAIREY SWORDFISH

-	L9730		Glen Callater. Complete in a heap. From Arbroath? *44/204801*	
15.12.40	K5949	767 Sqn	Glen Prosen. Mainly wing parts. Training flight from Arbroath. *44/323706*	S

GLOSTER METEOR

12.02.52	WA882	222 Sqn	Bennachie. Low-flying exercise from Leuchars. *38/663220*	S

GRUMMAN MARTLET

13.12.40	AL251	FLR	Ben Bheula. Abbotsinch/Donibristle. *56/157983*	M

HANDLEY PAGE HALIFAX

01.06.44	LL414	1667 HCU	Glen Isla. Cross-country from Sandtoft. *43/190740*	S

HAWKER AUDAX

05.05.39	K7376	8 FTS	Edendocher Hill. Local flight from Montrose. Two crew survived. *44/607853*	S
05.02.40	K7473	8 FTS	Cairn O'Mount. Montrose. *44/663806*	S

HAWKER FURY

18.01.38	K8263	8 FTS	Tipperweir Hill. Local flight from Montrose. Pilot survived. *44/69-86-*	S

HAWKER HENLEY

01.05.40	L3303	8 BGS	8 miles south of Huntly. Off track in bad visibility. Evanton. *37/?*	X

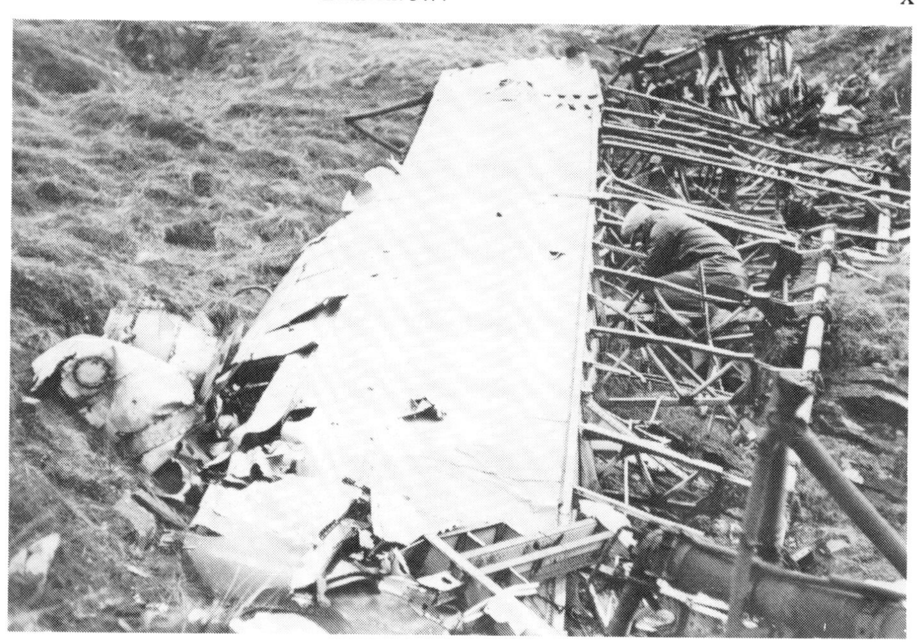

HAWKER HURRICANE

05.12.40	P3470		111 Sqn	10 miles north-west of Edzell. Ferrying Drem/Montrose. *44/?*	X
09.08.42	AG164		56 OTU	Near Loch Rannoch. Broke away from formation, possibly owing to lack of oxygen. Tealing. *42/?*	X
04.10.42	AF978		56 OTU	Wirren. Formation practice from Tealing. *44/52-73-*	X
21.04.43	V6938		56 OTU	Bawhelps. Local flight from Tealing. *44/230720*	S
19.11.43	BE651/ HV840		1 TEU	Cleish Hill. Formation practice, got into cloud and lost leader. Tealing. *58/08-96-*	X
06.02.44	LF160		516 Sqn	Near Kilchoan. On combined operations exercise from Connel. *47/464638*	S

HAWKER SEA FURY

| 17.09.53 | VW590/108-J | 811 Sqn | East Wirren. Arbroath. *44/558732* | S |

LOCKHEED 14

| 22.04.40 | G-AFKD | | Ben Uird. Perth/Heston. *56/40-98-* | S |

McDONNELL F-101 VOODOO

| 07.05.64 | 56-0013 | 81 TFW | Maol Odhar. Bentwaters. *49/883578* | S |

MILES MAGISTER

| 16.09.40 | T9814 | 19 OTU | 6 miles south of Dalwhinnie. Kinloss. *42/?* | X |

MILES MASTER

27.04.41	N7511	8 FTS	Forest of Birse. Lost in bad weather. Montrose. *44/53-91-·*	X
01.10.41	T8383	8 FTS	Pinderachy Hill. Navex from Montrose. *44/46-65-*	X
09.10.41	T8684	8 FTS	Cairn of Fingleny. Navex from Montrose. *45/615849*	M
17.01.42	AZ263	8 FTS	Tillentirk Hill. Navex from Montrose. *45/?*	X
18.03.43	DL415	2 FIS	Nathro Lodge. Navex from Montrose. *44/50-69-*	X
24.11.43	AZ333	2 FIS	Grampians. Cross-country from Montrose. Found 11.07.44. *44/?*	X

NORTH AMERICAN HARVARD

| 06.09.54 | KF177 | 3 FTS | Craigancash. Kinloss/Leuchars. *44/584775* | X |

NORTH AMERICAN F-86 SABRE

| 05.04.53 | XB610 | 147 Sqn | 7 miles north-east of Grantown-on-Spey. *36/?* | X |

NORTH AMERICAN F-100D SUPER SABRE

07.08.69	55-2817	48TFW	Peter Hill. Low-level cross-country from Lakenheath. Pilot ejected. *44/590900*	X

SUPERMARINE SCIMITAR

10.11.59	XD281/ ' 190-R	807 Sqn	Ben Vorlich. Pilot ejected. Lossiemouth. *57/620163*	S

SUPERMARINE SPITFIRE

10.03.41	X4647	58OTU	Ben Ledi. Lost without radio. Northolt/Grangemouth. *57/56-10-*	X
01.07.41	X4318	58OTU	Cloon. Grangemouth. *58/038047*	S
26.09.41	R6983	58OTU	Ben Gengie. Local flight from Grangemouth. *58/87-00-*	X
17.10.41	X4904	58OTU	Ochills. Formation practice from Grangemouth. *58/?*	X
05.11.42	R6886	8OTU	Glen Truim. Cockpit filled with smoke. Pilot baled out. Fraserburgh. *35/?*	S
10.11.42	X4487	8OTU	Glen Clova. *44/350700*	S
10.06.43	X4241	58OTU	Maddie Moss. Grangemouth. *58/93-01-*	X

VICKERS WELLINGTON

19.09.40	N2883	20OTU	Glen Moriston. Navex from Lossiemouth. *34/?*	X
23.10.40	L7775	20OTU	Bruach Mor. Misjudged position and let down too soon on navex from Lossiemouth. *43/089964*	S
13.02.42	T2707/ JM-Z	20OTU	Glen Affric. One engine failed, unable to maintain height over mountains at night. Crew baled out. Lossiemouth/Tiree. *34/076195*	M
14.11.43	L7867/ JM-J	20OTU	Ben Alder. Navex from Lossiemouth. Much of wreckage salvaged with pack mules. *42/480732*	S

WESTLAND WALLACE

03.09.39	K6028	9AOS	Benachie. Ferrying Evanton/Dyce. *38/668216*	M

Opposite: **Boeing B-29 44-62276 tail turret and tail bumper hydraulic ram on Glen Succoth. All twenty airmen on board were killed in this crash.**

Below: **Remains of BOAC Mosquito G-AGGF seen during 1975 on Glen Esk .**

Chapter Four

Southern Scotland

There are two notable concentrations of wrecks in this part of Scotland; the Mull of Kintyre and the Cairnsmore of Fleet. Both rear from the sea in ideal positions to trap unwary flyers and consequently became graveyards of aircraft. Another forbidding location lies to the west of Newton Stewart. It is wild, remote and beautiful but generally overlooked by people intent on speeding north to the Highlands. The long hikes to the wreck sites are amply rewarded by the scenery. The same can be said for the lonely rolling hills between the border and Edinburgh which include the Lammermuirs and the Moffat Hills.

Operational flying over the region was confined mainly to fighter squadrons based at Ayr, Drem, Abbotsinch and Turnhouse. A chain of airfields along the coast supported a variety of training activities safe from enemy interference but not from the effects of weather and high ground. Torpedo attack techniques were taught at Turnberry and Castle Kennedy, aerial gunnery at West Freugh, navigation at Wigtown and Dumfries, and Annan was a fighter OTU. RAF Dumfries doubled as an important MU and Aircraft Storage Unit.

Prestwick, perhaps the best-known Scottish airfield, was the terminal for a large proportion of all the thousands of aircraft ferried across the Atlantic for the RAF and USAAF. Although its weather record is excellent, there is much high ground in the vicinity and the tragic consequences of navigational errors can be seen to this day. Prestwick was still a useful staging point well after the war and the Invader on the Blackside Hills was on its way via Iceland to join the French Air Force. A Thunderbolt on the same hill was salvaged by the RAF after the USAAF found its heavy vehicles totally unsuitable for the job.

The huge bulk of the Cairnsmore of Fleet took a terrible toll of training aircraft, but unfortunately it is impossible to differentiate between the five Anson crashes as there are only sparse remains at the impact points. The impressive tail of the Heinkel 111 has now been recovered for preservation and much of the other wreckage was brought down by a USAF HH-53 helicopter when a memorial plaque to all the aircrew killed on the mountain was placed on the summit by the Dumfries and Galloway Aviation Group. The tail and undercarriage now reside with the North East Aircraft Museum at Usworth.

The Mull of Kintyre seems to have been another magnet for aircraft, lying as it did on navigation exercise routes and close to the anti-submarine bases in Northern Ireland. Long after the war it claimed two more Coastal Command aircraft, a Neptune and Shackleton. The latter was salvaged almost in its entirety but the Neptune was left more or less as it crashed with large sections strewn over the hill.

The hills to the east of Largs in Ayrshire are not particularly high but possess a surprisingly large number of crash sites. Potential investigators are warned that a compass is essential even on a clear day to identify the numerous small hills which all look alike. One of the most interesting relics up here was the fuselage of the Spartan Cruiser G-ACYK now in the Museum of Flight at East Fortune. Close to where the Cruiser crash-landed is a badly broken up Seafire and on Box Law an RAF Devon which, when seen in 1969 from the Viking wreck a mile away, appeared to be complete. It was only when we reached it that we found that the fuselage had been salvaged. The occupants of the Cruiser, Viking and Devon all escaped serious injury.

There were many collisions with the moorland around Lochwinnoch, but access was fairly easy and they were almost definitely removed. In the 'fifties I am told there was a Typhoon wing in use as a gate on a farm in this area. It may have come from DN365 but I am unaware of its exact location, assuming it still exists. Further north, near Greenock, an engine from the Anson on Dunrod hill forms a memorial at the Country Park Centre.

The mystery Fairchild Argus cockpit section in Southern Scotland still defies positive identification.

A wreck which still defies identification is a Fairchild Argus on a hilltop in the Moffat area. The cockpit structure and struts confirm the type and, according to local people, the occupants all escaped unscathed. It has been suggested that it was a civilian aircraft which crashed around 1950. RAF wartime records show no relevant Argus loss but it could also be a USAAF UC-61.

The ANEC Missel Thrush on Broad Law was a small low-winged monoplane which crashed on the Newcastle - Glasgow leg of the King's Cup Air Race, which in those days was a long distance affair. I am told that the engine remains on the mountain. The unknown wreck on Wester Dodd near Berwick may be Halifax JP190 of No.1656 HCU reported crashed on 'Wolf Cleugh Head' on 1 April 1944. I am unable to find this location on the OS Map so the connection remains unresolved. Another mystery surrounds the Seafire on Merrick. Contemporary newspapers report that it belonged to the Royal Canadian Navy but it would appear that this was pure conjecture.

ANEC MISSEL THRUSH

| 20.07.28 | G-EBRI | | Broad Law. Competitor in King's Cup Air Race. Cramlington/Renfrew. *72/15-24-* | S |

AIRSPEED OXFORD

| 15.03.42 | X7190 | 6 FPP | Near Wigtown. Ferrying Ratcliffe/Edzell. *83/?* | X |
| 17.08.42 | ? | TTU | Near Strathaven. Prestwick. *64/?* | X |

ARMSTRONG WHITWORTH WHITLEY

| 23.01.41 | P5041 | 502 Sqn | Mull of Kintyre. Became lost after convoy escort duty. Aldergrove. *68/597095* | S |

AUSTER WORKMASTER

| 18.10.63 | G-APMJ | | Dungeon Hill. Crosby-on-Eden/Campbeltown. *77/457862* | M |

AVRO ANSON

19.09.38	L7949	12 E&R FTS	Misty Law. Navex from Prestwick. *63/29-62-*	X
09.01.39	L9153	1 CANS	Rhinns of Kells. Night navex from Prestwick. *77/?*	X
26.07.39	K6255/ UA-A	269 Sqn	Dunrod Hill. Hit hill-top formation flying. Three survivors. From Abbotsinch. *63/237730*	S
17.04.42	W2630	1 OAFU	Cairnsmore. Navex from Wigtown. *86/?*	X
02.07.42	N5297	2 OAFU	Shalloch-on-Minnoch. Navex from Millom. *77/40-91-*	X
22.09.42	DJ126	9 OAFU	Cairnsmore. Navex from Llandwrog. *83/?*	X
23.10.42	DG787/J	ANBS	Corserine. Navex from Jurby. *77/497873*	S
03.02.43	N4995	1 OAFU	Cairn Hill. Navex from Wigtown. *76/?*	X
10.10.43	EF820	9 OAFU	Mull of Kintyre. Navex from Llandwrog. *68/?*	X
22.02.44	EG485/L1	10 OAFU	Cairnsmore. Navex from Dumfries. *83/?*	X
12.06.44	N9589	4 OAFU	Cairnsmore. Navex from West Freugh. *83/?*	X
09.07.44	N5140	1 OAFU	Knocktim, Cairnsmore. Navex from Wigtown. *83/50-64-*	X
21.07.44	MG356	4 OAFU	Bennanbrackle. Navex from West Freugh. *77/440775*	M
04.11.44	MG827	10 OAFU	Criffell. Navex from Dumfries. Crew survived. *84/953622*	M
06.12.44	EG693	2 OAFU	Craigronald. Navex from Millom. *83/523690*	M
01.02.45	NK945	45 MU	Turf Law. Kinloss/? *66/47-56-*	X

AVRO SHACKLETON

| 19.04.68 | WB833/T | 210 Sqn | Glenanuilt Hill. On exercise from Ballykelly. *68/649074* | S |

BLACKBURN BOTHA

| 02.03.42 | L6539 | 10 AOS | Cairnsmore. Navex from Dumfries. *83/?* | X |

BOULTON PAUL DEFIANT

29.08.41	T4042	60 OTU	6 miles north-west of Lauder. Loss of control in cloud. East Fortune. *73/?*	X
30.08.41	N1731	410 Sqn	Bleak Law. Training flight from Drem. *66/53-61-*	X
15.10.41	N1739	60 OTU	5 miles south of Gifford. Crew survived. East Fortune. *63/?*	X

BRISTOL BEAUFIGHTER

21.07.42	X7764	4 FPP	Auchingilloch. Ferrying Dumfries/Lossiemouth. *71/706360*	S
28.08.43	LZ156	304 FTU	Mull of Kintyre. Cross-country from Port Ellen. *68/624063*	S
30.10.43	LZ455	2 OAPU	Beinn Bhreac. Ferrying Filton to ? *68/615087*	S
03.05.45	NE813	132 OTU	Near Oldhamstocks. From East Fortune. *67/702699*	S

BRISTOL BEAUFORT

| 27.10.41 | L9817 | TTU | Knockside Hill. Torpedo exercise from Abbotsinch. *63/26-58-* | X |
| 02.09.42 | N1180/S | TTU | Tor Mhor. Exercise from Abbotsinch. *68/598079* | S |

BRISTOL BLENHEIM

08.11.39	P4848	SD Flt	Ben Inner. Perth/St Athan. *77/612968*	M
30.07.41	Z7646	18 MU	Blackhope Scar. Ferrying Haddington/Dumfries. *73/31-48-*	X
21.12.41	Z6350	5 AOS	Mull of Kintyre. Navex from Jurby. *68/?*	X
05.04.43	BA741	42 OTU	Near Peebles. Cross-country from Ashbourne. *72/?*	X
09.05.44	V5795	527 Sqn	Hart Fell. Inverness/Digby. *72/?*	

CONSOLIDATED CATALINA

| 30.12.42 | FP184 | 131 OTU | Smirton Hill. Navex from Killadeas. *76/12-79-* | S |

CONSOLIDATED B-24 LIBERATOR

31.08.41	AM915	BOAC	Achinoan Hill. Gander/Prestwick. *68/74-16-*	X
14.09.42	AL624	1653 HCU	Millfore. Training flight Prestwick/Burn. *77/471749*	M
13.06.45		448th BG	Pildinny Hill. Seething/Prestwick. *76/135775*	S

Opposite: **A typical Anson crash site, that of MG356 on Bennanbrackie, and** *below,* **fragments of Anson DG787 show where the aircraft hit the summit of Corserine in 1942.**

DE HAVILLAND DEVON
03.06.58   VP969   MCCF Box Law. Andover/Renfrew. *63/258607*   L

DE HAVILLAND DOMINIE
28.02.49   X7400   782 Sqn Dun Rig, Peebleshire. There are several mountains of this name! X

DE HAVILLAND DRAGONFLY
02.02.37   G-AEHC   Cairn Darnaw. Memorial at site. Renfrew/Speke. *77/516766*   S

DE HAVILLAND DRAGON RAPIDE
27.09.46   G-AFFF   Craigton Hill. Islay (Port Ellen)/Renfrew. *64/511769*   S

DE HAVILLAND DH 60 MOTH
26.09.36   G-ACGD   Broad Law. Edinburgh Flying Club, Turnhouse. *72/15-24-*   X

DE HAVILLAND MOSQUITO
21.01.44   DD795   60 OTU Corserine. Night navex from High Ercall. *77/504870*   M

DE HAVILLAND TIGER MOTH
10.01.39   L6932   12 E & R FTS Rhinns of Kells. Searching for a missing Anson. Crew uninjured
                                  and wreck salvaged. Prestwick. *77/?*
26.05.40   N9202   2 CPF Ladyland Moor. Abbotsinch. *63/30-59-*   X

DORNIER Do 217E-4
25.03.43   4365   7/KG2 Carnharrow. Based in Holland. *83/53-56-*   X

DOUGLAS HAVOC
03.08.41   AH463   14 FPP Near New Cumnock. Ferrying Abbotsinch/Burtonwood. *71/?* X

DOUGLAS B-26 INVADER
22.08.56   8811B   FAF Distinkhorn. Instrument let down into Prestwick from Keflavik
                                  on delivery. *71/594332*   M

DOUGLAS DAKOTA
10.04.47   K-14   RBAF Carlin's Cairn. Brussels-Evere/Prestwick. *77/498881/502882* M
28.03.56   G-AMRB   Starways Greenside Hill. Speke/Renfrew. *63/28-58-*   X

FAIREY BATTLE
29.09.41   L4997   10 AOS Lamb Hill. Loss of control in cloud. Dumfries. *78/954935*   S

FAIREY FIREFLY
26.10.44   DT977   1772 Sqn Blaeloch Hill. Training exercise from Ayr. *63/239550*   M
08.01.50   PP566/   1830 Sqn Meikle Bin. Local flight from Abbotsinch
           208-AC   *64/668822*   L

FAIREY FULMAR
07.07.41   -   804 Sqn Mull of Kintyre. HMS *Pegasus*/Northern Ireland. *68/?*   X

GENERAL DYNAMICS F-111E
19.12.79   68-0803   20 TFW Craignaw. Upper Heyford. *83/41-71-*   S

GLOSTER JAVELIN
21.11.60   XA825/K   29 Sqn Bowbeat Hill. Leuchars. *73/295475*   M

GRUMMAN WILDCAT
02.12.44   JV499   778 Sqn Blackside. Ayr/Abroath. *71/598298*   S

HANDLEY PAGE HALIFAX
01.04.44   JP190   1656 HCU Wolf Cleugh Head. near Berwick. Navex from Lindholme. *67/?* X

HANDLEY PAGE HAMPDEN
18.01.44   P1216   BTU   Braid Fell. Stalled, dived into ground. West Freugh. *82/11-67-*   X

HAWKER HIND
07.04.37   K6634   83 Sqn   Queensbury Hill. Cross-country from Turnhouse. *78/988997*   S
30.01.42   K6838   4 FPP   Eaglesham Moor. Ferrying Lossiemouth/Prestwick. *64/55-51-*   X

HAWKER HURRICANE
21.07.41   W9112   59 OTU   Lowther Hills. Crosby-on-Eden. *71/?*   X
13.09.43   KZ398/   186 Sqn   Shalloch-on-Minnoch. Training flight from Ayr.
            KZ674   *77/40-91-*   X
18.03.44   LD564   439 Sqn   Loch Doon. Dived out of cloud. Ayr. *77/73-92-*   S

HAWKER TYPHOON
24.01.42   DN365   187 Sqn   Near Lochwinnoch. Drem. *63/?*   X
20.02.44   R8971   439 Sqn   Benty Cowan. Ayr. *71/582090*   S
18.03.44   JR439   440 Sqn   Loch Skerrow. Squadron move Ayr/Woodvale. *83/578668*   M
27.03.45   MN532/FA-E   56 OTU   Stony Hill. Milfield. *71/729215*   M

HEINKEL He 111
09.08.40   -/   I/KG4   Eastmans Cairn. Operational sortie from Soesterberg, Holland.
            5J+SH   *83/497673*   S

JUNKERS Ju 88
25.03.43   144537/   II/KG6   Hare Hill. Probably cleared by 83 MU. Aircraft from Deelen,
            3E+HM   Holland. *65/17-62-*   X

LOCKHEED HUDSON
03.03.41   N7235   224 Sqn   Loch Bradan. Leuchars. *77/42-97-*   X
25.07.41   AE640   OADF   Feorlan, Mull of Kintyre. *68/639071*   X

Tailwheel assembly of Mosquito DD795 which hit Corserine whilst on a night intruder exercise from High Ercall in January 1944.

Part of the outer wing panel from Liberator AL624 on Millfore. The RAF roundel has faded to reveal the original USAAC star with red centre underneath.

LOCKHEED NEPTUNE
10.10.56   WX545/C   36 Sqn   Mull of Kintyre. ASR exercise from Ballykelly. *68/597096*   L

MILES MASTER
04.08.40   N7761   3 FPP   Burnhead. Ferrying Montrose/Reading. *77/06-14-*   X

McDONNELL RF-4C PHANTOM
28.03.79   68-0566   1 TRS/   Cairnsmore. Cross-country from Alconbury.
                        10 TRW   *83/49-67-*   S

NORTH AMERICAN HARVARD
16.01.53   FT401   22 FTS   Little Knock. Based at Syerston. *72/130263*   M

NORTH AMERICAN MUSTANG
10.04.43   AG386   268 Sqn   Near Bargrennan. Nominal base Snailwell. *77/?*   X

PERCIVAL PRENTICE
30.07.61   G-AOLR   Kilsyth Hills. Inbound to Renfrew. *64/682795*   M

PERCIVAL PROCTOR
01.10.50   G-AMAL   Near Peebles. Brough/Turnhouse. *72/?*   X

PIPER CHEROKEE
28.09.75   G-BATP   Bow Hill. Prestwick/Blackpool. *77/50-92-*   X

REPUBLIC P-47 THUNDERBOLT
??.12.43   USAAF   Distinkhorn. Prestwick? *71/59-33-*   S

SUPERMARINE SEAFIRE

| 14.09.45 | - | RCN? | Merrick. Allegedly from Anthorn. *77/42-85-* | X |
| 03.02.47 | PR432 | 804 Sqn | Hill of Stake. Found by shepherd 09.04.47. Donibristle/Eglinton. *63/274628* | M |

SUPERMARINE SPITFIRE

| 05.10.41 | R7152 | 58 OTU | Pentland Hills. Cross-country from Grangemouth. *72/?* | X |
| 17.02.43 | 'P6606' | 58 OTU | West Cairn Hill. Grangemouth. Quoted serial is incorrect. *72/11-58-* | X |

VICKERS VIKING

| 21.04.48 | G-AIVE | BEA | Irish Law. On Beam Approach to Renfrew from Northolt. All 20 on board escaped. *63/260593* | M |

VICKERS WELLINGTON

25.01.41	R1164	20 OTU	Box Law. Ferrying Kirkbride/Lossiemouth. *63/256609*	S
17.02.43	HX420	7 OTU	Glen Lussa. On torpedo exercise from Machrihanish. *68/74-27-*	X
27.02.43	HX779	7 OTU	Balnakeel Hill, Kintyre. Off course on flare-dropping exercise from Limavady. *68/?*	X
02.12.43	LB137	6 OTU	Mull of Kintyre. Navex from Silloth. *68/?*	X

De Havilland DH.90 Dragonfly G-AEHC, seen during its flying career, prior to its crash on Cairn Darnaw while en route Renfrew to Speke in 1937. A few pieces of wreckage can be found beside the memorial which marks the crash site.

Two views of a tailplane and elevator of Seafire PR432 recovered during 1986 from the Hill of Stake, where it crashed during February 1947 *(Max Elliott)*

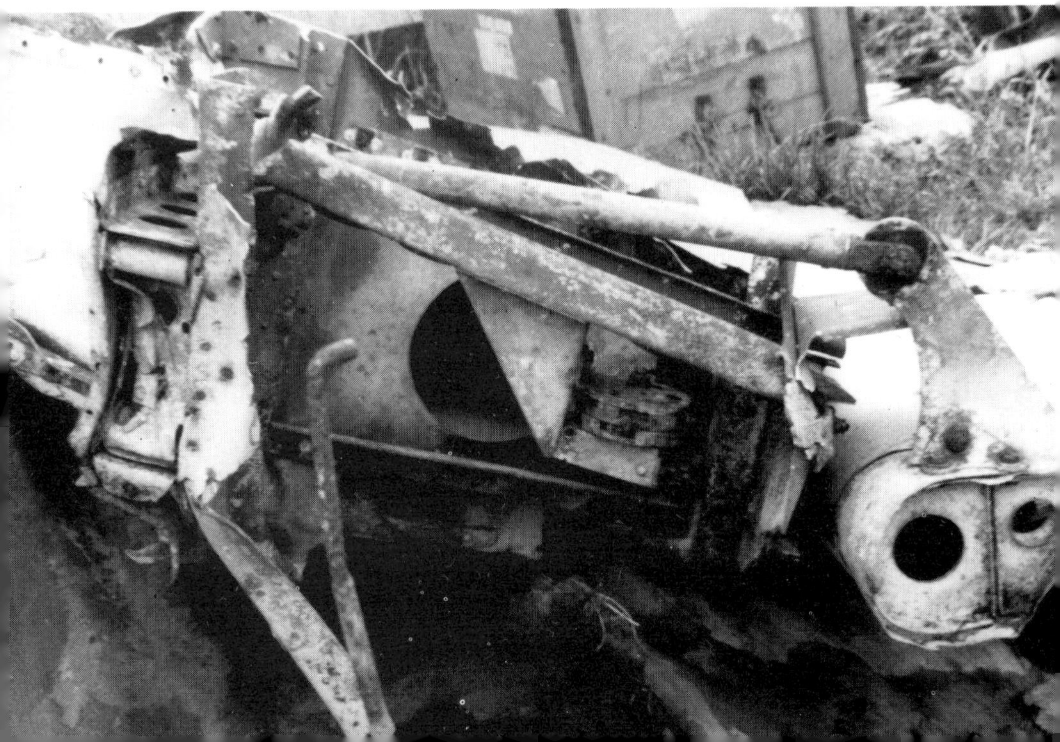

Chapter Five

Border Hills

As the chapter heading implies, this region straddles the border, although most of it is on the Scottish side. The Cheviot Hills are the dominant feature but there are many lesser heights which include the vast expanse of the Kielder Forest. Apart from the course of the Pennine Way, these hills are largely unfrequented by walkers and paths are few.

The wide valley of the Tweed was chosen for two aerodromes; Charter Hall and its satellite at Winfield. Night fighter crews were trained here on Beaufighters and Blenheims while, to the south of the Cheviots, their day fighter counterparts flew from Milfield, Brunton, Eshott and Acklington. Among the airfields built in the flat country around Carlisle were Crosby-on-Eden and Longtown which were used originally for day fighter training, then Coastal Command training on Beaufighters. There was an Elementary Flying Training School at Kingstown on the northern fringe of the city, at least two of its Tiger Moths being lost in high ground accidents.

The Halifax on Glendhu Hill is quite an interesting wreck, although not as intact as we were once led to believe. The reader is reminded that permission is required from the Forestry Commission to visit the site. Most of the crew baled out when an engine caught fire. The summit of The Cheviot is a large, flat, boggy area and happily the whole crew survived in two of the accidents up here. One involved a Stirling whose salvage must have been something of an epic as there is very little left of such a large aircraft. The same can be said for the nearby Anson which was carrying groundcrew and equipment during a squadron move.

The most celebrated Cheviot wreck is the B-17 on Braydon Crag, which was taking part in a raid on Ulm in Germany. Over the North Sea the weather failed to clear as forecast and the bomber force was recalled to its bases. The Cheviot aircraft became disorientated because of misleading signals from German decoy transmitters and flew around for several hours trying to get a position fix. The B-17 failed to clear the mountain in driving snow and two of the crew were killed instantly. Two local shepherds were subsequently awarded the British Empire Medal for their part in the search for the survivors and the dog belonging to one of them received the Dickin Medal, the animal VC.

The Lancaster on Mid Hill was returning from a raid on the submarine pens at Bergen but wandered off course with fatal results for the entire crew. Another operational loss was the Hampden which was homing to Waddington in Lincolnshire after a security patrol far out over the North Sea. The large remains of this aircraft are said to have been removed by helicopter about ten years ago but the RAF Museum have no knowledge of their preservation. Possibly they went to Otterburn to serve as targets on the ranges.

The Warwick on Cairn Hill was a surplus air-sea rescue aircraft which ironically was on its way to a Maintenance Unit for scrapping. Another unusual type this far north was a Mustang which crashed on a training flight from Yorkshire. The Bewcastle Fells were the scene of several crashes, but the exact positions are unknown. Somewhere in this area a Hurricane crashed in 1941, killing Prince Chirosakti of the Siamese royal family. A volunteer with the ATA, he was caught out by low cloud in a narrowing valley whilst ferrying the fighter from Kirkbride in Cumberland to Arbroath.

Simon Parry, author of *Intruders over Britain*, comments 'on the night of 24/25 March 1943, a total of eight Luftwaffe aircraft were lost on an extraordinary sortie over Northern Britain. Although some were credited to AA units, it seems likely that many simply flew into high ground.' One was the Ju88 on Linhope Rigg in the Cheviots, others included the Ju88 on Hare Hill, south of Edinburgh and the Do217 near Creetown, both being listed in the Southern Scotland section of this guide. The Do217 on Madam Law was shot down by a Beaufighter of No.68 Squadron.

ARMSTRONG WHITWORTH WHITLEY
15.10.40	P4952/	10 Sqn	Watch Crags. Lost, short of fuel returning to Leeming from operations. Crew baled out. *80/788823*	X

AVRO ANSON
05.03.40	N5094	49 Sqn	Cheviot. Unit move from Scampton to Kinloss. *81/912201*	S

AVRO LANCASTER
03.03.44	DS650	1666 HCU	1½ miles east of Catcleugh Reservoir. Loss of control in cloud on navex from Wombleton. *80/77-03-*	S
04.10.44	KB745/ VR-V	419 Sqn	Mid Hill. Returning to Middleton St George from operations to Bergen. *74/915215*	S

BOEING B-17G FORTRESS
16.12.44	44-6504	360th BS/ 303rd BG	Braydon Crag. Diverting to North Killingholme after aborted mission from Molesworth. 6 survived. *74/895214*	M

BOULTON PAUL DEFIANT
05.09.41	N1679	60 OTU	Dunmoor. Training flight from East Fortune. *81/956199*	S

BRISTOL BEAUFIGHTER
12.01.44	T5277	9 OTU	Bewcastle Fells. Practice controlled descent through cloud to Crosby-on-Eden. *86/?*	X
15.05.44	EL457	132 OTU	Hedgehope Hill. Night cross-country from E. Fortune. *81/94-19-*	X
18.11.44	T4772	9 OTU	Near Langholm. Crosby-on-Eden. *80/?*	X

BRISTOL BLENHEIM
30.08.38	K7067	90 Sqn	Cottonshopehead. Navex from Bicester. *80/78-01-*	X

DE HAVILLAND MOSQUITO
12.12.44	DD753	54 OTU	The Curr. On night exercise from Charter Hall. *74/850235*	M

DE HAVILLAND TIGER MOTH
01.03.43	N9462	15 EFTS	The Carts. Kingstown. *87/836730*	S
04.11.44	T6828	15 EFTS	Glendhu Hill. Kingstown. *80/58-86-*	X

DORNIER Do217E-4
24.03.43	5432/ U5+DL	3/KG2	Madam Law. Shot down by 68 Sqn Beaufighter during raid on Edinburgh. *74/865268*	S

HANDLEY PAGE HALIFAX
15.10.44	DK116/ GG-Z	1667 HCU	Glendhu Hill. Engine fire, some of the crew baled out. Sandtoft. *80/580862*	L
18.02.45	NR126	420 Sqn	Shill Moor. Returning to Tholthorpe from ops. *80/94-15-*	

HANDLEY PAGE HAMPDEN
| 18.03.40 | L4063 | 50 Sqn | Windy Gyle. Large sections removed possibly to Otterburn Ranges. Returning to Waddington from security patrol. *80/847158* | S |

HAWKER HART
| 10.10.39 | K6482 | 152 Sqn | Cheviots, 10 miles SW of Wooler. Turnhouse/Acklington. *80/?* | |

HAWKER HURRICANE
13.10.41	Z2349	3 Del Flt	Near Newcastleton. On ferry flight. *86/?*	X
03.11.41	Z3150/FT-V	43 Sqn	Peel Fell. Acklington. *80/62-00-*	X
16.03.42	P3902	59 OTU	Haggy Hill. Crosby-on-Eden. *79/28-85-*	X
26.02.43	P8813	55 OTU	Bewcastle Fells. Annan. *86/?*	X

JUNKERS Ju88
| 24.03.43 | 144354 | I/KG6 | Linhope Rigg. Code 3E+BH. From Deelen, Holland. *80/94-17-* | S |

MILES MASTER
| 29.09.41 | W8594 | 59 OTU | Tarnbeck Fell, Liddesdale. Crosby-on-Eden. *86/?* | X |

NORTH AMERICAN MUSTANG
| 19.02.43 | AG617 | 4 Sqn | Troughend Common. Navex from Clifton. *80/85-91-* | X |

PIPER CHEROKEE
| 13.02.79 | G-BHDG | | Hedgehope Hill. Edinburgh/Usworth. *81/94-19-* | X |

SHORT STIRLING
| 25.09.44 | EE972 | 1665 HCU | Cheviot. Navex from Tilstock. *81/915200* | S |

SUPERMARINE SPITFIRE
| 25.03.43 | P8587 | 57 OTU | Scald Hill. Eshott. *74/93-22-* | S |

VICKERS WELLINGTON
30.10.40	T2546	99 Sqn	Near Otterburn. Lost returning to Newmarket from ops. *80/?*	X
15.01.42	Z1078	150 Sqn	West Hill, Cheviot. Navex from Snaith. *74/894225*	M
01.03.43	R3173	15 OTU	Blackburn Fell. Dived into ground from cloud. Navex from Harwell. *80/80-93-*	X
28.10.45	LP665/C	105 OTU	Edges Green. Navex from Bramcote. *80/718687*	S

VICKERS WARWICK
| 23.07.46 | HG136 | 269 Sqn | Cairn Hill. Thornaby/Leuchars. *80/900195* | M |

Chapter Six

Western Pennines

Ranging from the high mountains of the north, such as Cross Fell and the Howgills, to the moorland of Lancashire, this region is far less popular with walkers than the Lake District or the Yorkshire Moors. Would-be investigators are warned that the hills in the north are extremely rough and pathless, which makes wreck hunting even more arduous than usual. This loneliness, however, is an added attraction. The moors further south are not so high or extensive, but in bad weather they can be just as hazardous to the inexperienced or ill-equipped.

Apart from those around Carlisle and the Solway Firth described in the Southern Scotland section, there were few other aerodromes on the fringes of this area of high ground. It was, however, criss-crossed with long distance navigation training routes and the so-called Barnard Castle Gap was often used by ATA ferry pilots who were not supposed to fly in or above cloud. Attempts to make it over the Pennines under a lowering cloud base brought death to several of them.

The best-known victim of a navex which went wrong was the Stirling on Mickle Fell, from which only the tail gunner survived. This wreck was one of the most intact in Britain until its recovery in 1980, but there is still quite a lot of wreckage overlooked or ignored at the time. A Mosquito crashed on Mickle Fell whilst engaged rather mysteriously in 'Cosmic Ray research', but I have not been able to locate its position.

Surprisingly little remains of the accidents on Cross Fell's large and lonely summit plateau and the salvage teams must have expended great efforts in re-covering them. The Spitfire on High Scald Fell a few miles away was the first of many lost to high ground during the type's service career. Another fighter, the Tomahawk on Red Gill Moss, was one of the initial batch for the RAF which in the panic after Pearl Harbor was taken over by the USAAF and then subsequently released to the British. It was on an army co-operation exercise when it crashed.

'Castle Moss' where a Botha from Millom crashed in 1941 is not shown on the one inch OS Map but it is believed to be south of the Tomahawk site by a few miles. Another mystery is the origin of the P-47 fragments on Pendle Hill. It could have come from Burtonwood, Warton or the training base at Atcham, near Shrewsbury.

The Halifax on Hoarside Moor had got lost on the way back from mine-laying near the Friesian Islands, but fortunately most of the crew survived. A memorial stone records the names of the crew of a Wellington on Anglezarke Moor. The pilot was thought to have lost control, possibly due to severe icing, and the aircraft sustained structural damage in the resulting high speed dive.

Several USAAF aircraft crashed in the south of the area, with three concentrated within a mile in the Trough of Bowland. The Liberator was on a training flight from Norfolk and must have been a combat veteran as it was described in USAAF terminology as 'war weary'. Close by, but two years before, a pair of P-38 Lightnings had flown into the hillside in cloud whilst on a practice flight from Goxhill on the south bank of the Humber. They belonged to the 78th Fighter Group which, when re-equipped with Thunderbolts, was to achieve a remarkable reputation flying escort missions from Duxford.

There are several other wrecks around the picturesque Trough of Bowland, but much of the moorland is private so it is essential to request permission to visit the sites. The unidentified C-54 was a Berlin Airlift aircraft and was en route to Burtonwood for overhaul when it wandered off course. A propeller blade was the largest part left on the fell but I believe this has now gone.

Winter Hill is reasonably close to roads and it seems certain that little or nothing is to be seen at the crash sites up here. It is known, for example, that Bristol Wayfarer G-AICS was recovered in 1958 after a crash which killed thirty-five people. A Chipmunk from Woodvale flew into the hill in cloud in the 'sixties and, although it finished up on its back, both occupants were able to extricate themselves and the aircraft was later removed.

AIRSPEED OXFORD
| 24.12.43 | BM837 | 410 Sqn | Winter Hill. Acklington. *109/66-15-* | X |

ARMSTRONG WHITWORTH WHITLEY
| 01.05.40 | K9039 | 51 Sqn | Burnside Fell. Crash-landing short of fuel. Dishforth. Returning from a raid on Fornebu, Norway. *103/67-53-* | S |
| 30.10.40 | P4957 | 10 Sqn | Near Slaggyford. Returning to Leeming from ops. *86/?* | S |

AVRO ANSON
07.01.42	R3409	1 AOS	Brant Fell. Navex from Wigtown. Aircraft iced up, crew baled out. *89/67-96-*	M
18.03.43	DJ453	4 AOS	Cross Fell. Navex from West Freugh. Aircraft iced up in cloud. All crew survived. *91/699345*	S
09.02.44	N4919	2 OAFU	Wolfhole Crag. Navex from Millom. Iced up and crash landed. All crew survived. *103/63-58-*	M
08.01.45	EF935	1 OAFU	Langdale Fell. Navex from Wigtown. *89/65-00-*	

AVRO TUTOR
| 15.01.40 | K3422 | 500 Sqn | Greenhill. Lost in fog, pilot baled out. Ferrying Linton-on-Ouse/Kirkbride. *86/650508* | M |

BLACKBURN BOTHA
| 22.08.41 | L6416 | 2 AOS | Castle Moss. Encountered bad weather on last leg of cross-country from Millom. *92/?* | X |

BLACKBURN SKUA
| 12.09.40 | 'L2629' | 4 FPP | Near High Bentham. Engine failure on ferry flight. Hullavington/Donibristle. Pilot baled out. | S |

BOULTON PAUL DEFIANT
| 18.08.41 | N1651/ JT-Z | 256 Sqn | Marshaw Fell. On training flight from Squires Gate. *102/60-52-* | S |

BRISTOL BEAUFIGHTER
| 04.07.43 | JM223 | 9 OTU | Croglin Fell. On practice controlled descent through cloud. Crosby-on-Eden. *86/60-49-* | X |

BRISTOL BLENHEIM
26.10.38	L1252/H	34 Sqn	Wemmergill Moor. Catterick/Kingstown	M
26.11.40	R3914/ YH-N	21 Sqn	Near Middleton-in-Teesdale. Lost returning from operational flight	X
09.08.44	BA246/14	12 PAFU	Bleasdale. Training flight from Woodvale. *102/582483*	M

CONSOLIDATED B-24J LIBERATOR
| 02.01.45 | 42-100322 | 715th BS/ 448th BG | Burn Fell. On training flight from Seething. *103/672533* | M |
| 19.02.45 | 42-50668 | 491st BG | Hameldon Hill. North Pickenham/Warton. *103/913306* | M |

CURTISS TOMAHAWK
10.02.43   AH744   1472 Flt   Red Gill Moss. On Army co-operation exercise from
Catterick. *92/876158*   M

DE HAVILLAND DRAGON RAPIDE
20.06.39   G-AERE   Langdon Common. Heston/Newcastle. *92/892321*   S

DE HAVILLAND DH 60 MOTH
21.04.36   G-AARE   Cross Fell. Engine only. Doncaster/Kingstown. *91/685344*

DE HAVILLAND MOSQUITO
05.01.50   VP199   109 Sqn   Mickle Fell area. Missing for some time. Coningsby. *92/?*   X

DE HAVILLAND TIGER MOTH
27.01.43   T5679   15 EFTS 6 miles south-west of Alston. Kingstown. *86/?*   X

DE HAVILLAND VENOM
04.03.57   WR557   22 MU   Croglin Fell. On test from Kirkbride. *86/640471*   L

DOUGLAS C-54 SKYMASTER
07.01.49   -   USAF   Stake House Fell. Berlin Airlift aircraft returning to
Burtonwood for maintenance. *102/556497*   S

DOUGLAS DAKOTA
10.01.46   KG502/A 1383 TCU Cold Fell. Night cross-country from Crosby-on-Eden. *86/588563* S
17.10.61   G-AMVC   BKS   Croglin Fell. Woolsington/Crosby-on-Eden. *86/599506* S

FAIRCHILD UC-61 FORWARDER
07.08.42   '41-54885'   5 ADG   Winter Hill. Believed cleared. *109/66-15-*   X

GLOSTER METEOR
22.03.54   WD778   228 OCU Knock Fell. Leeming. *91/723295*   L

HANDLEY PAGE HALIFAX
21.01.43   DT581   51 Sqn   Hoarside Moor. Returning to Snaith from mine-laying off
Friesian Islands. *103/935298*   L
12.04.44   BB310   1674 HCU Great Dun Fell. Navex from Aldergrove. *91/697324*   S
26.08.44   MZ658   431 Sqn   Allenheads. Mainly buried. Out of fuel, ex ops. Crew baled out.
Croft. *87/838506*   S

HANDLEY PAGE HAMPDEN
16.08.42   P4318   14 OTU   Arkengarthdale Moor. Navex from Cottesmore. *92/94-06-*

HAWKER HURRICANE
26.04.41   V7619   55 OTU   Allendale, Usworth. *87/?*   X
06.06.41   V6962   55 OTU   Langdon Common. Usworth. *92/883327*   S
18.07.41   V7534   59 OTU   Dufton Fell. Lost in bad visibility. Crosby-on-Eden. *91/73-28-* X
11.11.41   P3318   55 OTU   Waskerley Park Reservoir. Usworth. *92/02-44-*   S
28.04.43   P3901   55 OTU   Scarrowmanwick Fell. Annan. *86/61-47-*   X

LOCKHEED HUDSON
06.09.42   N7325/B59 1 OTU   Cross Fell. Silloth. *91/689331*   S

LOCKHEED P-38G LIGHTNING
26.01.43   42-12905/ 83th FS/ Dunsop Fell. Training flight from Goxhill.
             42-12928 78th FG *103/674541*   S

McDONNELL PHANTOM
20.01.72   XV477/C   6 Sqn   Thack Moor. Ran into cloud on low-level cross-country from
Coningsby. *91/613461*   S

MILES MASTER

| 19.12.41 | W8479 | | TFPP | Arant Haw Fell. Shawbury/Kirkbride. *89/662946* | S |
| 28.01.42 | T8614 | | 4 FPP | Beldoo Hill. Dumfries/Catterick. *92/885136* | S |

NORTH AMERICAN MUSTANG

29.11.42	AP208		4 Sqn	Holdron Moss. Cross-country from York. *103/609509*	S
04.06.44	-		496th FTG	Near Rochdale. Goxhill. *109/?*	X
17.08.44	AG443			Near Clitheroe. Hawarden. *109/?*	X
29.11.45	SR411		316 Sqn	Darwen Moor. *109/692191*	S

REPUBLIC P-47 THUNDERBOLT

| - | - | | USAAF | Pendle Hill. From Burtonwood?. *103/80-42-* | S |

SHORT STIRLING

| 19.10.44 | LK488/
QQ-E | 1651 HCU | Mickle Fell. Mostly recovered for RAF Museum. Night navex from Wratting Common. *92/812248* | S |

SUPERMARINE SPITFIRE

18.07.39	K9888		41 Sqn	High Scald Fell. Catterick/Kingstown. *91/708313*	S
14.05.41	P8161		9 MU	Near Colne. Ferrying from Cosford. *103/?*	X
27.03.42	P8463		81 Sqn	Near Stanhope. Lost formation in cloud. Turnhouse. *92/?*	X
16.07.42	W3628		315 Sqn	Wolfhole Crag. Woodvale. *103/63-58-*	S
28.12.42	AD230		317 Sqn	White Moss Fell. Woodvale. *102/58-50-*	

VICKERS WELLINGTON

| 20.08.42 | T2715/PP-E | 25 OTU | 14 miles south of Alston. Navex from Finningley. *86/?* | X |
| 16.11.43 | Z8799 | 28 OTU | Anglezarke Moor. On Bullseye Exercise, lost control in cloud, possibly due to icing. Wymeswold. Memorial nearby | S |

Curtiss Tomahawk AH744 on Red Gill Moss (*K. Haddleton*)

Fin from Stirling LK488 on Mickle Fell. Most of the aircraft's remains have subsequently been recovered for the RAF Museum.

Chapter Seven

Yorkshire Moors

Many bomber aerodromes were built in the Vale of York because of operational considerations, despite the high ground to the north, north-east and west. A small error of navigation while letting down at night, perhaps with flak damage and low on fuel, could be fatal. Most of the accidents on the moors thus involved bomber aircraft: Whitleys and Wellingtons in the early years of the war, later on, Halifaxes and Lancasters.

The network of roads and tracks over much of the moorland enabled crashed aircraft to be removed with relative ease, although parts were frequently buried on site. The more interesting wrecks therefore tend to be on the higher mountains on the eastern flank of the Pennines. These include Great Whernside and an entirely different summit twenty miles away confusingly known also as Whernside. Thanks are due to David Thompson of Stockton-on-Tees for his help in expanding the previous list for this area.

The two Dornier 217Es on 17 December 1942 were taking part in an intruder raid and ran into bad weather. The one on Wheeldale Moor was hit by AA fire after crossing the coast and apparently crashed whilst trying to land on the rough ground. The Junkers 88 on Eston Moor was engaged in a reconnaissance mission to Manchester when it was shot down by a Spitfire of No.41 Squadron, based at Catterick.

The largest group of sites is to be found on Great Whernside, but there is not much of any of the aircraft left owing to wartime salvage operations and subsequent amateur efforts. No.60 MU recovered most of the B-17 with the aid of a horse and sledge and were responsible also for clearing much of the widely-scattered Halifax wreckage. In July 1980, a local scout group carried a propeller down from the B-17 and it is now on display in Kettlewell where there is a memorial to the airmen killed on the mountain.

Some miles north of Great Whernside is Buckden Pike where a Wellington on a night cross-country flight crashed in January 1942. The crew were all Polish and the rear gunner, the sole survivor, later raised a memorial on the summit to his comrades. Another rear gunner escaped almost unhurt when a Wellington flew into Whernside. A few hundred yards away a Barracuda did the same thing just after the war, the pilot being lucky enough to walk away. Large parts of this aircraft were recovered for a now defunct air museum at York and their ultimate fate is unknown.

During the first years of the war, several Whitleys collided with the moors whilst returning from operations, three the same night on one occasion. The soft peaty ground was relatively yielding and happily many of the crews survived. The long trips in slow aircraft with minimal navigation aids took a heavy toll and one of the crashes occurred after a pilot fell asleep at the controls from sheer fatigue. Fortunately, he lived to tell the tale.

One of a number of wrecks on Arden Great Moor, the Spitfire, was returning to base after taking part in a Battle of Britain display at Acklington in September 1945 when it crashed in bad weather. The compact remains once included an almost intact wing, but the site was apparently cleared within the last ten years for reasons unknown. Perhaps it was reported by overflying aircraft? The Whitley in the same area had previously been abandoned by its crew when they ran out of fuel trying to find RAF Leeming after a raid on Stettin, a target which was at about the limit of this aircraft's range.

Anson K8778 of No.233 Squadron on Guisborough Moor the day after it crashed on 12 September 1937. Regrettably there is no trace of wreckage today. *(via David E. Thompson).*

AIRSPEED OXFORD

29.08.43	DF471	427 Sqn	Great Caum. Leeming/? *98/702828*	M
08.01.45	LW903	18 PAFU	Urra Moor. Transit flight Church Lawford/? *100/598012*	S

ARMSTRONG WHITWORTH WHITLEY

15.10.40	T4143	10 Sqn	Arden Great Moor. Returning to Leeming from ops, Stettin, out of fuel, crew baled out. *100/497935*	S
21.10.40	T4171/ GE-O	58 Sqn	Greenhow Moor. Returning to Linton-on-Ouse from ops. *93/598022*	S
23.08.41	T4234	10 Sqn	Widdale Fell. Returning to Leeming from ops. *98/804883*	S
28.03.42	Z9221	77 Sqn	Kirkby Malzard Moor. Bad weather forced early return to Leeming on ops. *99/17-75-*	X
28.03.42	-	51 Sqn	Great Whernside. Returning to Dishforth, ex-ops to St Nazaire. *98/005716*	S
28.03.42	Z9274/ MH-U	51 Sqn	Horncliffe Well. Returning to Dishforth ex-ops to St Nazaire. *104/129434*	S

AVRO LANCASTER

14.10.42	W4233	61 Sqn	Hagg House Moor. Returning to Syerston ex-ops to Kiel. *93/439995*	S
17.12.43	DS737/ EQ-C	408 Sqn	Murton Common. Believed cleared. Returning to Linton-on-Ouse ex-ops Berlin. *100/512882*	
17.05.44	-	419 Sqn	East Moors. *93/586928*	X
18.10.44	NF961	630 Sqn	Far Moor. Cross-country from East Kirkby. *100/493995*	S
05.11.45	RA571	429 Sqn	Beamsley Beacon. Cross-country from Leeming. *104/101523*	S

BOEING B-17G FORTRESS

17.05.45	44-8683	388th BG	Great Whernside. Navex from Knettishall. *98/003728*	S

BRISTOL BEAUFIGHTER

20.01.43	T5299	2 OTU	Near Huntersworth. Navex from Catfoss. *94/67-02-*	X
28.04.43	R2152	2 OTU	Waites Moor. Night navex from Catfoss. *94/658034*	S

BRISTOL BLENHEIM

21.03.40	L1117	219 Sqn	Kirbymoorside. Catterick. *94/61-00-*	X
18.07.41	L1449	54 OTU	Bransdale. Night Flying from Church Fenton. *94/604998*	S
??.02.42	-	54 OTU	Todd Intake Moor. Church Fenton. *93/599996*	S

DE HAVILLAND MOSQUITO

02.03.43	DD450	25 Sqn	White Crag. Holding for approach to Church Fenton. *104/068466*	S
08.11.46	NT266	54 OTU	Pockley Moor. Loss of control in cloud. Leeming. *94/618925*	M
13.12.48	RL197	228 OCU	Great Whernside. Training flight from Leeming. *98/000734*	S

DE HAVILLAND TIGER MOTH

06.09.45	N6793	4 EFTS	Spaunton Moor. Cross-country from Brough. *94/72-93-*	S

DORNIER Do 217E-4

17.12.42	4342/ U5+GR	III/KG2	Crow Nest. Raid on York from Deelen, Holland. *93/553914*	S
17.12.42	4348/ U5+AK	II/KG2	Wheeldale Moor. Raid on York from Deelen, Holland. *94/789984*	S

FAIREY BARRACUDA

15.12.45	DR306	769 Sqn	Whernside. Based at Rattray. Pilot unhurt. *98/743802*	M

GLOSTER JAVELIN

29.09.59	XA662/N	228 OCU	Apedale. Leeming. *98/017941*	M

HANDLEY PAGE HALIFAX

12.07.43	DG404	1663 HCU	Heathfield Moor. Navex from Rufforth. *99/11-67-*	S
23.11.43	DT578	1658 HCU	Great Whernside. Navex from Riccall. *98/001730*	S
31.01.44	DK185	1664 HCU	Black Beck Hole. On navex from Dishforth. *104/093467*	S
18.03.44	LL178	434 Sqn	Near Arden Hall. Croft. *100/505912*	S
28.01.45	LL576	1664 HCU	3 miles north-west of Pateley Bridge. One engine failed on navex from Dishforth. *99/?*	
-	-		Slipstone Crags. *99/138820*	S

HAWKER HURRICANE

22.04.40	L2009	11 Gp Pool	6 miles west of Ripon. Ferrying. *99/?*	X
10.01.41	P3522	213 Sqn	Caldbergh Moor. Leconfield. *99/10-83-*	X
19.05.41	P3772	55 OTU	Lockton Low Moor. Usworth. *94/850923*	S
14.06.41	V7024	55 OTU	Redshaw Moss. Usworth *98/81-84-*	X
12.06.42	AG680	5 FPP	Near West Keld. Ferrying Henlow/Silloth.	X

JUNKERS Ju 88A

30.03.41	-/ 4U+GH	1F/123	Eston Moor. Reconnaissance to Manchester, shot down by a Spitfire from 41 Squadron. *93/566171*	S

LOCKHEED HUDSON

11.02.40	N7294	220 Sqn	Warren Moor. Thornaby. *94/616083*	S
22.01.41	T9371	220 Sqn	Near Ingleby Arncliffe. Thornaby. *100/?*	X

NORTH AMERICAN MUSTANG

15.12.42	AG586	613 Sqn	Nr Pateley Bridge. Pilot baled out in bad weather. Ouston. *99/?*	S

PIPER CHEROKEE
23.09.69   G-AVYN   Ashfoldgill Beck. *99/078683*   M

SHORT STIRLING
14.08.44   EE975/   1660 HCU Old Cote Moor. Engine failure at night, unable to maintain
           GP-O   height. Most of crew baled out. *98/931741*   S

SUPERMARINE SPITFIRE
25.01.42   AD545   122 Sqn Spaunton Moor. Scorton. *94/?*   X
16.09.45   SM278/I4-F 567 Sqn Arden Great Moor. Acklington/Manston. *100/483935*   S

VICKERS WARWICK
13.11.43   BV336/MF-P 280 Sq Sneaton Low Moor. Thornaby. *94/895045*   S

VICKERS WELLINGTON
16.01.42   W5493   104 Sqn Arden Great Moor. Returning to Driffield from ops to Emden.
                                 100/495934   S
31.01.42   N2848/G   18 OTU Buckden Pike. Navex from Bramcote. Memorial on site.
                                 98/965784   S
03.09.42   Z8808   11 OTU Ashfold Gill Beck. Aircraft almost uncontrollable in bad weather.
                                 Crew survived. Bassingbourn. *99/077687*   S
03.09.42   DV718   11 OTU Blake Hill. Navex from Bassingbourn. Some wrckage recovered
                                 by South Yorks Air Museum. *98/024733*   M
12.02.43   BJ778/ZL-A 427 Sqn Black Intake Moor. Returning to Croft from ops. *100/581997*   M
21.04.44   BK347   30 OTU Whernside. Off track on navex from Hixon. *98/743817*   S
28.05.45   HE226   17 OTU Bycliffe. On navex from Silverstone. *98/013687*   S
   -          -   Brayshaw Scar. *98/925726*   S

WESTLAND LYSANDER
14.01.41   T1689   4 Sqn Ilkley Moor. Lost in bad weather on ferry flight to or from
                                 Clifton. *104/11-46-*   X

Opposite: The impact point on Far Moor where Lancaster NF961 crashed on 18 October 1944. The photo was taken in 1974 since which time most of the debris has been cleared. (*David E. Thompson*)

Above: Halifax DG404 which came down on Heathfield Moor, seen at Speke, just off the Rootes production line. (*via P. Summerton*)

Below: Cowling rings and tubing from Wellington BK347 on Whernside.

Chapter Eight

Lake District

On the coastal plain to the north-west of the Lakeland Fells lay the Maintenance Unit airfields of Silloth and Kirkbride, the former in its early years doubling as a Coastal Command Hudson OTU. In the south there were three training aerodromes; an Air Gunners School at Barrow, an Observer School at Millom and at Cark an organisation for teaching instructional techniques, the Staff Pilot Training Unit. Aircraft from the Observer Schools at Dumfries and Wigtown frequently overflew the area, as did Wellingtons from the Bomber OTUs in the Midlands.

It will come as no surprise to learn that Ansons were the most common casualties on the fells, at least thirteen being lost here. On a terrible night of thunderstorms in August 1943, No.10 (O) AFU at Dumfries lost no less than three of them. The next morning found search aircraft combing the Irish Sea for survivors. The wrecks were discovered eventually on the fells, a few of the crewmen having survived.

The remains of three veteran biplanes can still be seen, the earliest being the Vildebeeste and Hind which crashed in June 1937 and the Hawker Hector as late as 1941. The latter was being ferried to the MU at Dumfries when the engine failed, the pilot being killed in an attempt to crash-land amongst the rocks of Red Pike. The occupants of the DH.86 which force-landed on Bolton Ground were fortunate to escape serious injury.

Pieces of Avenger are still embedded in Great Gully above Wastwater, but the battered engine which lay on the lake shore now seems to have gone. There has been much 'tidying up' by the National Park authorities in recent years and wreckage at some sites near popular walking routes has been buried or removed.

Perhaps the most interesting site is on Great Carrs where a Halifax hit the summit and was later pushed over the cliffs into Broad Slack by the salvage crew. Much of its remains lie here to this day and most walkers are familiar with this wreck, although few are aware of the story behind it and generally assume that it is a Lancaster. The circumstances are yet another minor tragedy of the Second World War, all seven crew being killed in the accident. Completely lost on a night cross-country through inexperience, the pilot descended below safety height hoping to break cloud and pinpoint his position.

On two separate occasions, pairs of Hurricanes from No.55 OTU hit high ground in formation. There is little left of any of them, most of the wreckage of those on Slight Side being covered by rocks. In March 1941, two Hurricanes from No.601 Squadron on a transit flight were also lost after becoming separated in a snowstorm. Another fighter, this time a Spitfire, went missing on 20 November 1947 and was found by a shepherd on Scafell on 1 May of the following year.

An unusual aircraft was the US Navy Skyraider on Banna Fell. The crew escaped serious injury and the wreckage was later buried. Some years later, a Canadian Sabre hit Iron Crag, leaving a long trail of debris. The fin with squadron badge was reputed to be there but no-one seems to have located it. Another post-war crash involved a USAF Beech Expeditor light transport which ran into a blizzard. Both occupants struggled down the fell after a cold night sheltering in the fuselage.

A perennial mystery no nearer to solution is the identity of an aircraft which crashed on the Old Man of Coniston on 14 October 1942. The records of RAF Millom say it was a 'Lockheed aircraft', whilst those of RAF Ayr, from which it departed, quote it as a 'Beechcraft Twin'. It was being flown from Ayr to Limavady in Northern Ireland by two American civilian ferry pilots employed by the Lockheed Corporation. It may have been a Beech C-45, the type later to be known as the Expeditor.

The Cumbrian Fells are very steep and craggy and particularly dangerous in mist, although on the credit side there are plenty of well-worn paths. The famous series of guides to the Lake District written by A. W. Wainwright are a recommended source of information on routes, a few of the wrecks being mentioned. The Oxford on Caw Fell, for example, is described picturesquely in his inimitable fashion as 'ruins of aeroplane'!

AIRSPEED OXFORD

02.11.41	AT486	2 AOS	Caw Fell. Navex from Millom. *TM/131106*	M

AVRO ANSON

20.09.42	N4869/60	2 OAFU	Muncaster Fell. Navex from Miloom. *TM/12-99-*	X
01.10.42	DJ410	4 AOS	Green Gable. Four of crew survived. Navex from West Freugh. *TM/213107*	S
01.01.43	AX145	1 OAFU	Frozen Fell. Navex from Wigtown. *TM/287335*	S
01.01.43	W2629	1 OAFU	High Pike. All crew survived. Night navex from Wigtown. *TM/32-35-*	X
14.02.43	DJ466/BP	10 OAFU	Grisedale Pike. Navex from Dumfries. *TM/198236*	S
08.04.43	EG361/D3	5 AOS	Lords Seat. Navex from Jurby. *TM/204266*	S
09.08.43	DJ222	10 OAFU	Green Gable. Night navex from Dumfries. *TM/215107*	S
09.08.43	N5053	10 OAFU	Great Dod. Night navex from Dumfries. Four of the crew survived. *TM/344205*	S
09.08.43	DJ275/AL	10 OAFU	Sca Fell. Night navex from Dumfries. *TM/209061*	S
30.01.44	MG393	AN & BS	Starling Dod. Night navex from Jurby. Descended through cloud when fuel almost exhausted. *TM/144157*	S
20.03.44	EG686	SPTU	Swirl How. Navex from Cark. *TM/278002*	M
17.11.44	MG464/J	AN & BS	Grisedale Pike. Navex from Jurby. Caught in downdraught. *TM/197219*	S
02.01.45	LT741/5	10 AGS	Black Combe. Apparently entered cloud on gunnery exercise from Barrow. *TM/140859*	S

BEECH C-45 EXPEDITOR

12.03.47	-	USAF	Black Combe. Crew escaped. Prestwick/Bovingdon. *TM/131856*	M

BOEING B-17E

14.09.43	41-9051	92nd BG	Skiddaw. Training flight from Alconbury. *TM/258286*	S

BRISTOL BEAUFIGHTER

15.11.43	EL285/E	9 OTU	Wolf Crag. Night flying from Crosby-on-Eden. *TM/353223*	S

CESSNA 150E

22.02.66	G-ASYH		Black Combe. Blackpool/Newcastle. *TM/13-85-*	S

DE HAVILLAND DOMINIE

30.08.46	X7394	782 Sqn	Broad Crag. Abbotsinch/Stretton. *TM/218078*	M

DE HAVILLAND MOSQUITO

10.04.45	HK141	51 OTU	Catstye Cam. Night navex from Cranfield. *TM/346151*	S

DE HAVILLAND DH.86B

28.07.39	L7596	24 Sqn	Bolton Ground. Hendon/Sydenham. Forced-landing. *TM/24-83-*	X

DH.86A L7596 shortly after its forced landing on Bolton Ground, had previously seen civilian use as G-ADYJ *(via David E. Thompson)*

DOUGLAS SKYRAIDER
02.10.53	132370	USS *Wasp*	Banna Fell. Mainly buried. USS *Wasp* (in Irish Sea)/Prestwick. Crew survived. *TM/106174*	S

ENGLISH ELECTRIC CANBERRA
20.01.58	WT505	58 Sqn	Ponsonby Fell. Site virtually cleared. Wyton. *TM/085070*	S

GENERAL DYNAMICS F-111E
05.03.75	68-0081	20 TFW	Ulthwaite Rig. Upper Heyford. *TM/518094*	S

GRUMMAN AVENGER
16.01.45	JZ390	763 Sqn	Great Gully, Wastwater. Engine now in lake. On night navex from Inskip. *TM/148038*	S

HANDLEY PAGE HALIFAX
24.01.44	JP182	ATA	Eel Crag. Two ferry crew killed. *TM/193204*	S
22.10.44	LL505	1659 HCU	Great Carrs. Became completely lost on navex from Topcliffe. *TM/270009*	L

HAWKER HECTOR
08.09.41	K8096	1 SAC	Red Pike. Ferrying Binbrook/Dumfries. *TM/168105*	M

HAWKER HIND
05.06.37	K6614	98 Sqn	Thornthwaite. West Freugh/Hucknall. *TM/428106*	M

HAWKER HURRICANE
31.03.41	V7539	601 Sqn	Scar Crags. Flying with V6987 from Northolt to Crosby-on-Eden. Got lost in blizzard. *TM/213205*	M
31.03.41	V6987/ UF-L	601 Sqn	Birk House Moor. Northolt/Crosby-on-Eden. *TM/366170*	S
12.08.41	V6565/ V7742	55 OTU	Slight Side. Operational training from Usworth. *TM/211049*	M
20.07.42	R4217	55 OTU	Dowthwaitehead. Cross-country from Usworth. *TM/37-21-*	X
21.01.43	AF959	55 OTU	Great Calva. Cross-country from Annan. *TM/286316*	X
23.04.43	AG264/ AG275	55 OTU	Brim Fell. Much of one of the aircraft is in Low Water. Annan. *TM/273991*	S

Above: **Dominie X7394 'Merlin V' of the Royal Navy's 782 Squadron, which was to be lost on 30 August 1946 and,** *below* **the remains of the same aircraft amongst the rocks on Broad Crag during June 1969.**

LOCKHEED HUDSON
10.11.42   AM680   1 OTU   Beda Head. Mainly buried. Navex from Silloth. *TM/427171*   S

MILES HAWK TRAINER
22.09.52   G-ALGJ   Lank Rigg. *TM/088123*   S

NORTH AMERICAN F-86 SABRE
26.06.59   23380/   421 Sqn/ Iron Crag. Prestwick/Wethersfield. *TM/121120*   M
            BB-380   RCAF

PIPER CHEROKEE
17.09.66   G-ASEK   Esk Hause. Milfield/Newcastle. *TM/23-08-*   S

PIPER SARATOGA
29.11.87   G-BNYS   Bow Fell. Staverton/Prestwick. *TM/24-06-*   X

SUPERMARINE SPITFIRE
20.11.47   SL611   603 Sqn Sca Fell. Wreckage found by shepherd. 01.05.48.
                                Hawarden/Turnhouse. *TM/21-07-*   X

VICKERS VILDEBEESTE
04.06.37   K4607   42 Sqn   Crinkle Crags. Filton/Donibristle. *TM/254053*   S

VICKERS WELLINGTON
08.02.42   T2714/   22 OTU   Burn Tod. Crashed after radio failure on navex from Wellesbourne
            DD-C   Mountford. *TM/287330*   S
16.12.42   X3336   23 OTU   Carlside. 48 miles off track on night navex from Pershore.
                                TM/246288   S
16.06.44   HZ715   22 OTU   Red Pike. Navex from Wellesbourne Mountford. *TM/159156*   X

Below: **The tangled remains of Hawker Hector K8096 on Red Pike, which crashed following engine failure during a ferry flight to the MU at Dumfries in 1941.**

Chapter Nine

Isle of Man

The Isle of Man wreck sites have not been covered in the previous editions of this book and the present list consists mainly of approximate locations gleaned from official records. I and a few other people have found several of the sites and the map references are given where known. Since the island's hills are neither very high nor very extensive, it was a relatively easy task to recover the debris. Much of it found its way to a dump at RAF Jurby. It seems certain, however, that there are at least a few fragments to be found at most of the sites.

Apart from Jurby which housed an air navigation and bombing school, there were two other Manx wartime aerodromes. Andreas was built as a fighter base but with the Luftwaffe rarely seen over the Irish Sea after 1941, it was downgraded to an air gunners school. Ronaldsway, which is now the island's airport, was a grass field until rebuilt later in the war for Fleet Air Arm torpedo training. Few of the crashed aircraft originated locally, however; the mountainous island, often wreathed in cloud, was at the cross-roads of many navigational training routes from airfields on the mainland and was an ever-present hazard to aircraft in transit between England and Northern Ireland.

There were at least two crashes on the South Barrule, but I could find nothing during a wide search. The North Barrule, in contrast, has much evidence on its slopes, the most melancholy being the crater made by a Fortress on 23 April 1945. The death toll of thirty-one was the second highest suffered in any high ground crash in Britain up to the present day. For the record, the worst was the Bristol Wayfarer accident on Winter Hill in Lancashire on 27 February 1958 when thirty-five of the forty-two on board lost their lives. The aircraft, G-AICS, was flying from Ronaldsway to Ringway.

Another Fortress hit a hill near Spanish Head on 14 April 1945 but the site was close to habitation and was cleared without difficulty. Other American losses were two Liberators on ferry flights from support bases in Northern Ireland and a Marauder in which six of the eight on board were killed. One of the Liberators flew into the summit of Snaefell, as did a Wellington in October 1941. With a railway to the top and a road nearby, the wreckage was soon removed but doubt, some pieces may have been overlooked.

It was the humble Anson which suffered most, no less than fifteen coming to grief on the island hills up to 1961. Their relatively low cruising speed saved many airmen and on one occasion in November 1944 and Anson night-flying from Millom ended up on Snaefell with no injury to her crew. A badly injured wireless operator who had crawled from an Anson wreck on Slieu Ruy in January 1946 was found by a dog which alerted its master.

Regrettably, the island continued to take a toll of aircraft after the war, one of the largest being a Halifax of Lancashire Aircraft Corporation in 1948. It was taking part in an airlift of milk from Ulster to the mainland to relieve a shortage and failed to clear the summit of Cronk Ny Arree Laa by only a few feet. A patch of bare earth strewn with small pieces marks the spot and, half a mile away, some spars from Rapide G-AIUI are built into a dry-stone wall.

On the steep seaward slopes of the same hill, a Cherokee crashed in 1982 in approximately the same position as the wartime Marauder. The following year, a Hawk from Valley became the North Barrule's eighth victim. It remains to mention an unidentified crash on Beinn-Y-Phott Mountain which was attended by Jurby's ambulance crew on 8 August 1944. Two men were rescued and two bodies removed so it was probably yet another Anson.

AVRO ANSON

01.08.40	L7963	SAN	Dalby Mt. Navex from St Athan. All crew survived. *95/24-78-*	X
17.01.42	N5030	27 OTU	Snaefell. Navex from Lichfield.	X
13.02.42	AX411	5 AOS	Glen Mona. Navex from Jurby. All crew survived. *95/44-89-*	X
13.02.42	N5346	5 AOS	North Barrule. Navex from Jurby.	X
17.07.42	R9640	SPTU	North Barrule. Navex from Cark.	X
19.08.42	N4902	2 OAFU	Snaefell. Navex from Millom.	X
16.12.42	R3432	10 AOS	Snaefell. Navex from Dumfries.	X
03.05.43	R9604	4 AOS	South Barrule. Navex from West Freugh.	X
13.06.44	EG233	1 OAFU	North Barrule. Navex from Wigtown.	X
01.08.44	EG437	3 SGR	Slieau Ouyr. Navex from Squires Gate. *95/43-88-*	X
13.11.44	AX177	1 OAFU	Cronk Ny Arree Laa. Navex from Wigtown.	X
15.11.44	EG416	2 OAFU	Snaefell. Navex from Millom. All crew survived.	X
03.01.46	MG445	5 ANS	Slieau Ruy. Navex from Jurby. *95/44-87-*	X
05.09.53	VM418	1 ITS	Clagh Ouyr. Millom/Jurby. *95/41-89-*	X
20.02.61	VL312	TTCCF	North Barrule. Wyton/Aldergrove	X

BAe HAWK

24.06.83	XX166	4 FTS	North Barrule. Low-level navex Valley/Lossiemouth	X

BOEING B-17G FORTRESS

23.04.45	43-38856		North Barrule. 31 killed. Ridgewell/Nutts Corner. *95/442908*	S

CONSOLIDATED B-24 LIBERATOR

09.06.44	42-51202	311th FYS	Snaefell. Ferrying Langford Lodge?/Mainland.	S
06.07.44	42-50762		North Barrule. From or to Langford Lodge. *95/433904*	X

DE HAVILLAND DRAGON RAPIDE

15.08.47	G-AHKR	Greeba Mt. Speke/Ronaldsway. *95/321813*	X
10.06.48	G-AIUI	Cronk Ny Arree Laa. Elmdon/Ronaldsway. *95/225748*	X

HANDLEY PAGE HALIFAX

28.09.48	G-AJNZ	Cronk Ny Arree Laa. Nutts Corner/Speke. *95/223746*	X

HANDLEY PAGE HAMPDEN

01.01.40	P1260	7 Sqn	Snaefell. Navex from Upper Heyford.	X

LOCKHEED HUDSON

09.09.41	N7337	1 OTU	North Barrule. Navex from Silloth.	X
21.09.42	AM608/B77	1 OTU	Slieu Freoaghane. Navex from Silloth. *95/34-88-*	X

Above: **Crater and scattered wreckage where Fortress 43-38856 flew into the North Barrule, with a tragic loss of 31 lives.**

MARTIN B-26 MARAUDER

04.07.44	41-35791	449th BS/	Cronk Ny Arree Laa. Northern Ireland/		
		322nd BG	Andrews Field?		X

PIPER CHEROKEE

30.10.82	G-DJMS		Cronk Ny Arree Laa. Newtonards/Ronaldsway	X

SUPERMARINE SPITFIRE

14.12.43	EN856	303 Sqn	Snaefell area. Training flight from Ballyhalbert.	X

VICKERS WELLINGTON

08.10.41	Z8424	8 FPP	Snaefell. Ferrying. Hawarden/Aldergrove.	X
23.12.44	MF174	EANS	South Barrule. Navex from Shawbury.	X

Chapter Ten

Peak District

The name of this area conjures up an image of jagged mountains but is very misleading as it consists entirely of moorland up to about 2,000 feet with some rocky outcrops and cliffs, the so-called edges. The heights can be treacherous in winter and even in summer when mist descends. Much of the Peak is private land and only the 2½ inch OS shows which this is. I have, therefore, deleted certain map references to avoid conflict with land owners. Access to the moors is restricted on up to twelve days during the grouse-shooting season, August 12 to December 10.

Ron Collier of Glossop has published two books about the Peak wrecks which tell survivors' stories and include much information about each incident. One wreck which continues to elude researchers is the Mill Hill Liberator. Reputedly, there were only two on board (a ferry crew?) and both survived. There is also a rumour that it was stolen from Burtonwood early in 1945 but this seems unlikely.

The other Liberator in the Peaks is now known to be a US Navy PB4Y-1 which became completely lost with radio failure whilst returning from an anti-submarine patrol out of Dunkeswell in Devon. The crew baled out over Lincolnshire and luckily the aircraft ran out of fuel over the moors before it reached Manchester.

The V1 flying bomb on Margery Hill consists of a large crater and a few scraps of metal, all that remains of a weapon air-launched from a Heinkel 111 off the East Coast. It was one of a number aimed at Manchester on Christmas Eve 1944 but few reached their target. There is rumoured to be a German bomber somewhere in the same area which was shot down during a raid on Sheffield. Many years ago. a friend of mine found a 13 mm cartridge case of German origin on these moors.

A concentration of interesting wrecks can be found in the vicinity of Higher Shelf Stones within easy reach of the Snake Pass road. The photo-reconnaissance version of the Superfortress had once served with the 509th Composite Group, the unit responsible for the atomic bomb attacks on Japan. A Canadian Lancaster crashed about three years before, but there is little sign of the aircraft today. Strewn down Ashton Clough are the substantial remains of a C-47 which was carrying a jeep, as springs and transmission parts have been found here.

An element of mystery surrounds the Defiant on Bleaklow as bullet holes were found in the wreckage. It may have been shot down but it seems more likely that it simply flew into high ground, perhaps after a brief skirmish with an enemy aircraft which had strayed into its path. The Botha nearby was a brand new aircraft on a delivery flight.

Shining Tor is close to the Cat and Fiddle Inn on the Macclesfield to Buxton road on which the crew of a Defiant were found wandering one morning. They were somewhat dazed, having flown into the hill in the dark at an angle flat enough for the fighter to remain in one piece. The same squadron, No.96 at Cranage near Middlewich, had already lost another Defiant in the Peaks when the engine failed at night and the crew had to take to their parachutes.

On the southern fringe of the Peak is the striking ridge known as The Roaches. There were several crashes here but it is reasonably accessible and only fragments are left. Investigators should not be surprised if they encounter a wallaby on this hill; they were introduced to the area many years ago as an experiment and there is now a thriving colony!

A number of aircraft returning from bombing operations crashed in the Peaks. The most northerly was the Pathfinder Mosquito on its way back from Hamburg to its base near Cambridge. Lost and circling on one engine, trying to find their position, the crew were unlucky enough to fly into a cliff face. The crew of a Wellington belonging to a Canadian squadron were more fortunate when the aircraft bounced to a halt on a flat portion of Blackden Edge. They had been on a raid over Lorient in Occupied France and were heading for base in North Yorkshire. A Wellington of No.150 Squadron crashed on Upper Tor whilst coming back from a Belgian target. It was not far from the spot where a Heyford came down before the war.

AIRSPEED CONSUL

12.04.51	TF-RPM		Outer Edge. Delivery flight Croydon/Prestwick/Iceland. *TM/175996*	S

AIRSPEED OXFORD

18.10.43	LX518	17 PAFU	Margery Hill. Navex from Wheaton Aston. *TM/180968*	S
12.03.44	LX745	17 PAFU	Shining Tor. Cross-country from Calveley. *TM/99-73-*	S
14.04.45	L4601	17 SFTS	Shutlingsloe. *TM/97-69-*	S
29.12.45	HN594	21 PAFU	Brown Knoll. Navex from Seighford. *TM/082852*	S

AVRO ANSON

31.03.42	N9912	25 OTU	Whitwell Moor. Navex from Finningley. *TM/249976*	S
11.12.44	N9853	16 SFTS	Edale Moor. Navex from Newton. *TM/102883*	S
23.11.45	NL185	Bmbr Cmnd HQ Flt	The Cloughs. Halton/Feltwell. *TM/089867*	S

AVRO LANCASTER

03.01.45	NF908	467 Sqn	The Roaches. Training flight from Waddington. *TM/002636*	S
18.05.45	KB993/EQ-U	408 Sqn	Jame's Thorn. Local flying from Linton-on-Ouse. *TM/080946*	S
21.12.48	PA411/A3-U	230 OCU	Tintwhistle Knarr. Training flight from Lindholme. *TM/035992*	S

BLACKBURN BOTHA

10.12.41	W5103	7 FPP	Bleaklow. Delivery flight Sherburn-in-Elmet/Hawarden. *TM/110972*	M

BOEING B-17G FORTRESS

06.04.45	43-37667	709th BS/ 447th BG	Meltham Moor. Training flight from Rattlesden.	M

BOEING F-13A SUPERFORTRESS

03.11.48	44-61999	16 PR Sqn	Higher Shelf Stones. Named 'Over Exposed'. Scampton/ Burtonwood. (*TM/091947*	X

BOULTON PAUL DEFIANT

13.04.41	N1766	96 Sqn	Rowlee Pasture. Engine failure at night. Crew baled out. Cranage. *TM/151905*	S
29.08.41	N3378	255 Sqn	Bleaklow. Believed shot at in error by a Spitfire and damaged. Hibaldstow/Turnhouse. *TM106957*	M
16.10.41	T3921	96 Sqn	Shining Tor. Local flying from Cranage. Crew survived. *TM/998738*	S

BRISTOL BLENHEIM

30.01.39	L1476	64 Sqn	Sykes Moor. Familiarisation flight from Church Fenton. *TM/080970*	L

CONSOLIDATED B-24 LIBERATOR

10.11.44	42-94841	857th BS/ 492nd BG	Twizle Head Moss. Training flight from Harrington.	S
-	-	USAAF	Mill Hill. *TM/058906*	L

255 Squadron Defiant N3378 rear fuselage on Bleaklow in April 1975. This item has since been recovered for preservation.

CONSOLIDATED PB4Y-1 LIBERATOR
19.12.43   63934   VB-110   Irontongue Hill. Radio failure, lost returning after anti-sub patrol from Dunkeswell, diverting to Beaulieu. Crew baled out. *TM/017009*   M

DE HAVILLAND CANADA CHIPMUNK
03.07.51   WB579/16   22 RFS   Arnfield Moor. Local flight from Barton. *TM/025946*   S

DE HAVILLAND CANADA L-20A BEAVER
05.12.56   52-6145   81st FBW   Bramah Edge. Burtonwood/Sculthorpe. *TM/050975*   S

DE HAVILLAND DRAGON RAPIDE
30.12.63   G-ALBC   Kinder. Caught in downdraught. Middleton St George/Manchester. *TM/102883*   S

DE HAVILLAND MOSQUITO
22.10.44   PF396/   571 Sqn   Dean Rocks. Lost returning on one engine to Oakington from
        8K-K   raid on Hamburg. *TM/026032*   S

DE HAVILLAND TIGER MOTH
12.04.45   T6164   24 EFTS   Blindstones Moss. Cross-country from Sealand. *TM/035016*   S

DE HAVILLAND VAMPIRE
25.07.51   WA400   102 FRS   Strines Moor. Forced-landing, short of fuel. North Luffenham. *TM/22-89-*   S
08.08.57   XE866   4 FTS   Moscar Moor. Descending through cloud. *TM/220857*   S

DOUGLAS DAKOTA
19.08.49   G-AHCY   BEA   Wimberry Stones. On instrument approach. Nutts Corner/Ringway. *TM/014025*   S

DOUGLAS C-47A SKYTRAIN
24.07.45   42-108982/J   314 TCG Jame's Thorn. Amiens/Prestwick. *TM/082946*   L

FAIREY BARRACUDA
25.07.45   MD963 NAS Dunino Standedge. Pilot was from Donibristle Ferry Pool. *TM/103023* S

FAIREY SWORDFISH
25.01.40   P4223   819 Sqn Heydon Head. Missing for a month. Silloth/Ford. *TM/084048* S

FIESELER FZG.76 (V1)
24.12.44   -   Margery Hill. Air launched towards Manchester by He 111 off
                            East Coast. *TM/185966*   S

GLOSTER METEOR
12.04.51   WA791/   66 Sqn Sliddens Moss. Linton-on-Ouse. *TM/069029*   L
          VZ518

HANDLEY PAGE HALIFAX
05.10.43   HR727   51 Sqn Ashop Moor. Lost, short of fuel returning to Snaith from
                            ops to Frankfurt. *TM/130877*   S

HANDLEY PAGE HAMPDEN
23.05.40   L4055/OL-B 83 Sqn Dearden Moss. Returning Scampton from ops.   S
21.01.42   AE381   50 Sqn Cluther Rocks. Lost on cross-country from Skellingthorpe.
                            TM/078875   S

HANDLEY PAGE HEYFORD
22.07.37   K6875   166 Sqn Broadlee Bank Tor. Night exercise from Leconfield. *TM/111860* S

HAWKER HURRICANE
22.02.45   PZ765/   11 PAFU Tintwhistle Knarr. Formation practice from Calveley.
          PZ851/   *TM/040993*   S
          PZ854

The mystery American Liberator on Mill Hill. A wing section with retracted
undercarriage is among the larger pieces of wreckage.

De Havilland DH.89A Rapide G-ALBC wreck on Kinder Scout soon after its demise in 1963. *(Sheffield Newspapers, via T. Allonby)*

LOCKHEED P-38J LIGHTNING
10.05.44   42-67207 496th FTG Tintwhistle Knarr. Training flight from Goxhill. *TM/040993*   S

MILES HAWK TRAINER
28.07.57   G-AJSF   Kinder Low End. Squires Gate/Barton. *TM/074863*   S

MILES MASTER
15.01.43   W8840   7 FPP Near Leek. Ferrying   X

NORTH AMERICAN HARVARD
30.11.44   FT442   5 PAFU Shining Tor. Cross-country from Tern Hill. *TM/002738*   S
14.01.52   FT415   22 FTS Wool Packs. Syerston/Kemble. *TM/090868*   S

NORTH AMERICAN MUSTANG
30.05.45   44-72213   Castleshaw Valley. *TM/998107*   S

NORTH AMERICAN F-86 SABRE
22.07.54   XD707/730   66 Sqn Ashop Moor. On an exercise from Linton-on-Ouse.
                                  TM/072902   L
14.12.54   -   RCAF Holme Moss. North Luffenham/Ringway. *TM/090050*   S

REPUBLIC P-47C THUNDERBOLT
25.04.43   41-6227/   78th FG Rushup Edge. Loss of control in cloud flying Speke/Horsham
            UN-F   St Faith. *TM/093845*   S

60

5 PAFU Harvard FT442, from Tern Hill, pictured soon after its crash on Shining Tor.

SHORT STIRLING
21.07.44   LJ628   1654 HCU Upper Commons. Navex from Wigsley. *TM206959*   M

SUPERMARINE SEAFIRE
16.07.49   SP314/325 1831 Sqn Wildboarclough. Formation flight from Stretton. *TM/99-67-*   S

SUPERMARINE SPITFIRE
17.11.40   P7593   4 FPP The Roaches. Ferrying Kirkbride/West Malling. *TM/00-63-*   X

VICKERS WELLINGTON
31.07.41   W5719/   150 Sqn Upper Tor. Became lost returning to Snaith after abandoning
          JN-S   raid on Cologne owing to bad weather. *TM/111876*   S
26.01.43   X3348   427 Sqn Blackden Edge. Returning to Croft from ops to Lorient. All
                            crew survived. *TM/128876*   S
30.01.43   R1011   28 OTU Birchen Bank Moss. Navex from Wymeswold. *TM106987*   S
22.10.52   MF627   6 ANS Rod Moor. Navex from Lichfield. *TM/26-88-*   S

WESTLAND LYSANDER
19.08.41   V4903   6 AACU Chew Reservoir. Flew reciprocal on night exercise from
                            Sealand. *TM/04-01-*   X

Chapter Eleven

North Wales

Although dominated by Snowdonia, North Wales possesses a number of outlying ranges of considerable magnitude. They include the Berwyns, the so-called Harlech Dome, the Arans and Cadair Idris and its extensive foothills. There are also the many areas of high moorland, the most dangerous to aircraft being Minera Mountain which rises steeply from the edges of the Cheshire and Shropshire Plains.

The few wartime airfields were confined to Anglesey and the coastal strip. Valley was and still is the most important, doubling as a fighter station and Transatlantic Terminal for the USAAF. Mona and Bodorgan were the other Anglesey aerodromes, the former teaching air gunnery and later, navigation, the latter supplying towed targets for local ranges. Towyn was another target towing aerodrome and Llanbedr, built as a fighter base, became an Armament Practice Camp for fighter squadrons.

It was from Llandwrog and Penrhos, however, that most of Snowdonia's victims originated. Penrhos, near Pwllheli, had been a pre-war bombing school and Llandwrog, close to Caernarfon, became its satellite, although planned as a forward fighter station. The roles were later reversed with Llandwrog becoming the parent aerodrome, both concentrating on the training of navigators for Bomber Command.

Despite being far away from significant interference by the Luftwaffe, it was not a happy choice of locations from which to allow trainee navigators to learn by their mistakes. Many of the exercises were carried out at night, often in poor weather, with tragic results. Soon, as a warning to the pupils, there was a map in the control tower at Llandwrog liberally sprinkled with red crosses, each marking an Anson crash in the mountains. So numerous were the accidents, not only to locally-based aircraft but to strangers as well, that a mountain rescue unit had to be formed and became the model for many similar units within the RAF.

The Fortress in the Berwyns was probably the first aircraft of its type lost in the UK by the 8th Air Force and the one near Barmouth amongst the last. An aircraft which almost came to grief in the Berwyns was a USAAF C-47 which bent *both* wingtips on a mountain top but managed to limp to RAF Montford Bridge in Shropshire for a wheels-up landing.

A particularly tragic incident was the loss of a formation of three Spitfires on a training flight from Llanbedr. In the same area, Wellington R1068 of No.21 OTU crashed on 17 August 1941 and its crew are commemorated on a plaque at Pennal Church. There seems to be no trace of the accident on nearby Rhos Fach Mountain, however. Other memorials in North Wales can be found in the Llanberis Pass in remembrance of the Marauder crew on Y Garn, on the summit of Arenig Fawr where a Fortress crashed on a night practice flight, and on Moelfre above Penmaenmawr at the point where a Liberator hit the mountain.

On the Carnedd Range there was a large concentration of crashes and, such is the spread of wreckage, it is often difficult to establish the identity of the aircraft from which they came. Llyn Dulyn - the Black Lake - and its immediate surroundings, became notorious as a graveyard of aeroplanes. The wing centre section from a USAAF C-47 was a grim landmark for decades until it was dislodged from the cliff to join the rest of the aircraft in the lake. Since the second edition of this guide appeared, many of the aircraft engines have been removed from Snowdonia by helicopter in a misguided tidying-up operation. The only consolation is that thay have gone to museums, but they would have been better left as memorials.

For an absorbing account of the stories behind the crashes in Snowdonia, the reader is recommended to obtain a copy of Edward Doylerush's book *No Landing Place*, also published by Midland Counties Publications. Eddie has contacted many of the survivors, analysed the possible causes, and described how the rescue services developed. A sequel covering crash sites in other parts of North and mid-Wales is now in preparation.

It should be emphasised that the whole expanse of Snowdonia and its outliers is potentially dangerous to the unwary walker. In winter, conditions can be suicidal and bad weather can be encountered at any time of the year, often with little pre-warning. On Minera Mountain there is an extra hazard in the form of old unfenced mine shafts.

The Dulyn C-47 in 1944 *(W. W. Harris)*

AIRSPEED OXFORD

03.08.41	N4568	11 SFTS	Sychnant Pass. Solo flight from Shawbury. *115/757769*	S
15.11.42	BM824	11 PAFU	Berwyn Mts. Navex from Shawbury. *125/?*	X
20.02.44	X7064	11 PAFU	Moel-y-Gamelin. Night cross-country from Calveley.	S
13.01.45	LB537	418 Sqn	Cornel. 50 miles off course. Found by shepherd 05.02.45. Blackbushe/Squires Gate. *115/703670*	S

ARMSTRONG WHITWORTH WHITLEY

26.09.42	BD232	24 OTU	Foel Fras. Night cross-country from Honeybourne. *115/703671*	M

AUSTER AOP.6

21.10.56	VF554/G	663 Sqn	Bera Mawr. Operating on exercise from landing strip at Aber. *115/679689*	M

AVRO ANSON

07.09.41	N9617	10 OTU	Berwyn Mts. Navex from Abingdon. *125/?*	X
07.01.42	N9562	9 AOS	Cwm Silyn. Navex from Llandwrog. *115/51-50-*	S
20.04.42	N4980	9 AOS	Foel Fras. Navex from Llandwrog. Three survived. *115/69-67-*	X
21.08.42	N4966/R4	2 SAN	1 mile west of Garth. Navex from Cranage. *117/?*	X
20.11.42	N4981	9 OAFU	Moel Eilio. Navex from Penrhos. *115/55-58-*	S
28.11.42	DJ635	9 OAFU	Foel Gron. Night navex from Llandwrog. *115/56-56-*	X
13.01.43	EG110	9 OAFU	Foel Grach. Navex from Llandwrog. Two survived. *115/69-66-*	S
23.08.43	N5371/AK	9 OAFU	Foel Fras. Navex from Llandwrog. All crew survived. *115/699678*	X
05.10.43	LT184	7 AOS	Mynydd Perfedd. Navex from Bishops Court. *115/626622*	S
08.11.43	N9855	3 OAFU	Pen yr Ole Wen. Night navex from Halfpenny Green. *115/660622*	S
20.11.43	MG111	9 OAFU	Cwm Silyn. Navex from Llandwrog. *115/520507*	S
30.11.43	EF909/J3	5 AOS	Foel Grach. Night navex from Jurby. All crew survived. *115/691667*	X
20.02.44	LT433/MI	SPTU	Llyn Cowlyd. Navex from Cark. Four of the crew survived. *115/727636*	S
25.04.44	AX583	2 OAFU	Drum. Navex from Millom. *115/715698*	S
08.06.44	LT116	9 OAFU	Mynedd Perfedd. Navex from Llandwrog. *115/625623*	S
13.06.44	EG472/CW	9 OAFU	Moel Hebog. Night navex from Llandwrog. One survived. *115/568470*	M
12.07.44	MG804	8 OAFU	Foel Fras. Night navex from Mona. Four crew survived. *115/699675*	X
11.08.52	VM407	23 MU	Snowdon. Aldergrove/Llandow. *115/607548*	S
20.05.59	VV955	CCCS	Tal-y-Fan. Diverting to Valley during flight Bovingdon/ Ballykelly. *115/722722*	M

AVRO LANCASTER

16.11.42	W4326	101 Sqn	Dolwen Hill. Navex from Holme-on-Spalding Moor. *125/955095*	M
06.02.45	NE132	1653 HCU	Rhinog. Broke up in CuNim cloud on navex from North Luffenham. *124/632285*	M

AVRO LINCOLN

15.03.50	RF511	230 OCU	Cwm Llafar. Navex from Scampton, diverting to Valley. *115/679638*	M

BLACKBURN BOTHA

23.08.42	L6318	3 SGR	Tal-y-Fan. Navex from Squires Gate. *115/72-72-*	S
28.08.43	L6202/6-20	11 RS	Llwydmor. Training flight from Hooton Park. *115/683694*	M

BLACKBURN SKUA

19.02.41	L3054	801 Sqn	Elidir Fach. West Freugh/St Merryn. *115/611615*	S

Above: The remains of 24 OTU Whitley BD232 close to Llyn Dulyn, Snowdonia, lost during a night cross-country flight from Honeybourne in September 1942.

Below: One of the many Anson crashes in Snowdonia is illustrated by the spar and undercarriage remains of MG804 on Foel Fras, the crew being lucky to survive.

BOEING B-17 FORTRESS

11.08.42	41-9098	340th BS/	Cadair Bronwen. Training flight from Grafton Underwood.	
		97th BG	*125/079342*	S
04.08.43	42-3124	303rd BG	Arenig Fawr. Night training flight from Molesworth.	
			125/826369	S
08.06.45	44-6005	511th BS/	Craif Cwm Llydd. Polebrook/Valley.	
		351st BG	*124/645122*	S

BRISTOL BEAUFIGHTER

08.09.41	X7640	2 FPP	Moel Siabod. Ferrying Weston/Sealand. *115/714552*	S
03.11.43	NE203	2 FPP	Worlds End. Ferrying Weston/Sealand. *117/243483*	S
10.02.45	RD210	1 FU	Aran Fawddwy. Fuel consumption test from Pershore.	
			125/863225	M

BRISTOL BLENHEIM

23.03.40	L4873	90 Sqn	Foel Wen. Cross-country from Upwood. *125/102324*	M
09.04.40	L9039/	13 OTU	Craig Yr Ysfa. Cross-country from Bicester.	
	LD-Y		*115/694638*	M
31.03.43	V6099	13 OTU	Marchlyn Mawr. On cross-country from Bicester. Not found	
			for twelve days. *115/609621*	S

CESSNA 310

29.09.68	G-ARMK		Carnedd Dafydd. Leavesden/Squires Gate. *115/667628*	S

CESSNA 337

08.06.79	G-ATNY		Moel Siabod. Coventry/Ronaldsway. *115/706545*	S

CONSOLIDATED B-24J LIBERATOR

07.01.44	42-99991		Moelfre. Named 'Batchelor's Baby'. Transit flight Valley/	
			Watton. 6 survived. *115/716746*	S

DE HAVILLAND MOSQUITO

09.02.44	LR412	540 Sqn	Aran Fawddwy. Cross-country from Benson. *125/859213*	M
25.09.44	HX862	60 OTU	Drum. Night navex from High Ercall. *115/716692*	M
01.11.44	W4088	51 OTU	Mynydd Mawr. Night navex from Cranfield. *115/543552*	M
31.07.48	TV982	502 Sqn	Snowdon. In thunderstorm. Horsham St Faith/	
			Aldergrove. *115/609528*	M

DE HAVILLAND QUEEN BEE

24.02.42	V4793	1 AACU	Snowdon. Got out of radio control on pilotless flight from	
			Bodorgan. *115/599553*	S

DE HAVILLAND VAMPIRE

07.11.51	WA305	202 AFS	Near Ruabon. Valley. *117/?*	X
19.04.56	VV601	7 FTS	Llyn Cowlyd. Local flying from Valley. *115/72-66-*	X
12.10.56	VZ874/19	7 FTS	Mynydd Mawr. Night flying from Valley. *115/539547*	X
18.04.66	5C-YA	Austrian AF	Mynydd Tarw. Test flight from Hawarden. *125/11-32-*	S

DOUGLAS BOSTON

17.10.42	Z2186	418 Sqn	Carnedd Dafydd. Cross-country from Bradwell Bay.	
			Pilot survived. *115/667629*	S

DOUGLAS C-47 SKYTRAIN

24.08.42	-	60 TCG	Moel Morfydd. Prestwick/Atcham with personnel for the	
			14th FG. *117/16-46-*	S
12.11.44	43-48473	27 ATG	Craig-y-Dulyn. Diverting to Valley due to fog.	
			Le Bourget/Burtonwood. *115/698667*	S

ENGLISH ELECTRIC CANBERRA

09.12.57	WK129	RRE	Carnedd Llwelwyn. Trials from Pershore. *115/685647*	M

FAIREY BATTLE

16.02.41	L5755	HQSFP	Berwyn Mts. *125/?*	X

Above: **Beaufighter RD210 was lost while on a fuel consumption test from Pershore. Here its tail and rear fuselage lie embedded in a gully on Aran Fawddwy** *(A. W. Evans)*

Below: **13 OTU Blenheim L9039 wedged in the cliffs of Craig-y-Ysfa** *(E. Doylerush)*

FAIREY FULMAR
05.02.41   'N4074'   Minera Mountain. *117/262511*   S

GRUMMAN AVENGER
03.02.44   FN821/4K   848 Sqn   Trum-y-Fawnog. Gosport/Machrihanish. *125/013257*   S

HANDLEY PAGE HALIFAX
03.09.44   JD417   1656 HCU   Yr Eifl. Navex from Lindholme. *123/365448*   S
                                 116/072768   S

HAWKER HART
12.02.37   K4931   5 FTS   Minera Mt. Grantham/Sealand. *117/?*   X

HAWKER HENLEY
17.10.40   L3351   1 AACU   Yr Eifl. Towyn. *123/36-44-*   S
20.11.42   L3334   1605 Flt   Cwm Silyn. Target-towing from Towyn. *115/516502*   S

HAWKER HURRICANE
28.01.42   V7001   TFPP   Minera Mt. Ferrying Hanworth/Hawarden. *117/?*   S
09.08.42   P3385   MSFU   Allt Fawr. Speke/Valley. *115/681468*   X

HEINKEL He 111H-5
14.04.41   F4801/   3/KG 28   Llwydmor. Raid on Barrow-in-Furness from Nantes.
           IT+EL   *115/684698*   S

JODEL DR.250
22.08.69   G-AVIV   Carnedd Dafydd. Off course Birmingham/Dublin. *115/664629*   S

LOCKHEED HUDSON
04.02.43   AM832   1 OTU   Llechog. Night navex from Silloth. *115/596537*   S

LOCKHEED P-38F LIGHTNING
0?.0?.42   14th FG?   Berwyn Mts. From Atcham or High Ercall. *125/038295*   S

LOCKHEED VENTURA
18.08.43   AE688/   464 Sqn   Carnedd Dafydd. Night cross-country from Sculthorpe.
           SB-Q   *115/659629*   S

MARTIN B-26G MARAUDER
01.02.45   44-68072 Unassigned   Y Garn. Ferrying St Mawgan/Burtonwood. Wreckage scattered
                                  down Cwm Cwyion from ridge. *115/628598*   S

MILES MASTER
30.10.40   N7442   5 SFTS   Minera Mt. Sealand. *117/266493*   S
28.07.43   AZ714   17 PAFU   Rhobell Fawr. Cross-country from Calveley. *124/79-26-*   S

NORTH AMERICAN HARVARD
19.03.51   FX249   502 Sqn   Hope Mt. *117/280584*   S

NORTH AMERICAN P-51D MUSTANG
05.05.45   FX898   61 OTU   Minera Mt. Cross-country from Rednal. *117/239463*   S
17.05.45   44-726844 335th FS/   Arran Fawddwy. Dived out of formation probably due to
           4th FG   oxygen starvation. Debden   S

PIPER TWIN COMANCHE
22.10.72   G-AVFV   Crib-y-Ddysgyl. Southend/Valley. *115/61-55-*   S

REPUBLIC P-47 THUNDERBOLT

04.05.44	42-75101	495th FTG	Mynydd Copog. Dived into high ground. Atcham. *125/884143*	M
08.07.44	41-6195/ VM-C̄	552nd FTS/ 495th FTG	Denbigh Moors. Pilot baled out in spin. Atcham. *116/916593*	S
16.09.44	41-6246	495th FTG	Aran Fawddwy. Found by a shepherd a week later. Atcham. *125/862222*	M
0?.0?.44	-	495th FTG	Glyndyfrdwy. Atcham. *125/151409*	S

SUPERMARINE SPITFIRE

26.05.41	R6834	57 OTU	Cwm Cwmorthin. Apparently descended through cloud. Hawarden. *115/67-46-*	S
26.09.41	X4843	57 OTU	Yr Aran. Hawarden. *115/605517*	S
16.11.41	X4713	57 OTU	Ruabon Mt. Local flight from Hawarden. *117/?*	X
05.04.42	X4239	57 OTU	Cwm Barlwyd. Operational training from Hawarden. *115/71-48-*	S
22.10.42	BL518 BM573 R7296	41 Sqn	Tarrenhendre. Training flight from Llanbedr. *135/68-04-*	S
14.12.42	P7295	61 OTU	Cadair Bronwen. Cross-country from Rednal. *125/076337*	S
31.08.45	TE210	631 Sqn	Worlds End. Llanbedr. *117/242489*	S

VICKERS WELLINGTON

06.04.42	P9299	1429 Flt	Nr Llanymawddwy. Cross-country from East Wretham. *125/?*	X
28.05.42	HX433	1443 Flt	Mynydd Moel. Fuel consumption text from Harwell. *124/73-13-*	S
19.07.42	DV800	27 OTU	Black Ladders. On navex from Lichfield. *115/675635*	S
13.02.43	HE466	30 OTU	Foel Grach. Night cross-country from Hixon. *115/692664*	S
20.11.43	LB185	3 OTU	Moel Y Croesau. On navex from Haverfordwest. *124/747386*	S

WESTLAND LYSANDER

| 15.12.42 | T1655 | 61 OTU | Cadair Bronwen. Caught in downdraught while searching for missing Spitfire. Rednal. *125/078342* | S |

Undercarriage leg of Boston Z2186 near summit of Carnedd Dafydd (*E. Doylerush*)

Above: **Wing section from the Carnedd Dafydd Boston Z2186** (*E. Doylerush*)

Below: **An engine from the Martin Marauder 44-68072 on Y Garn** (*E. Doylerush*)

Chapter Twelve

Mid and South Wales

The presence of a Spitfire OTU at Llandow to the west of Cardiff led inevitably to high ground collisions as trainee pilots got lost or wandered into cloud. One of them, X4913 in the Brecon Beacons, has the unfortunate distinction of being the longest-missing aircraft in Britain's hills. It disappeared on 3 November 1941 and was discovered by a farmer rounding up his sheep on 10 July of the following year. This assumes of course that no other wreck lies undiscovered somewhere in the wilder parts of the Scottish Highlands - an unlikely possibility, however.

Virtually the whole of the area is mountainous, the Brecon Beacons being the most formidable of a series of ranges which stretch from Plynlimon south to the Black Mountains. The lesser heights of the Prescelli Mountains in the south-west are a further hazard to aircraft. The airfields were necessarily confined to the coast and the gentler countryside of Pembrokeshire. To the west, Aberporth was used by target-towing aircraft for the local ranges, there were Coastal Command fields at Carew Cheriton, Dale, Talbenny, St Davids and Brawdy, and training aerodromes at Haverfordwest and Templeton.

Fairwood Common was built as a fighter station for the defence of South Wales. It was supported by Pembrey which later became an Air Gunners School. There was a similar school at Stormy Down, near Porthcawl and towards Cardiff the MUs at St Athan and Llandow. RAF Madley was just across the border in England but close enough to the mountains to ensure that it was often responsible for dealing with crashes.

The Bomber OTUs in the South Mid-lands tended to send their pupil crews over the same standard cross-country routes night after night in all weathers. One of those flown by No. 22 OTU at Wellesbourne Mountford in Warwickshire used a turning point at Fishguard. The track crossed a lot of inhospitable country and at least two of the unit aircraft came down in the mountains. One was Wellington MF505 on Carreg Goch and a memorial plaque lists the names of the crew. Another memorial can be found near where Wellington R1465 crashed in the Beacons during a night navex. In Glyntawe churchyard is a commemorative inscription dedicated to the help rendered by the villagers in searching for the survivors of an Anson crash in 1939.

I did not include the Plynlimon F-5 Lightning (the photo-reconnaissance version) in the previous editions of this book as it was very accessible, as well as substantially complete, and I feared it would be removed piecemeal. This seems to have happened anyway although happily most of the large sections have found their way to museums. The serial number is still unknown as it was not painted on the fins and rudders, but the large code letters 'G2-Q' were visible on the underside of one of the wings. Up to about ten years ago, the Lightning was one of the most intact wrecks in Britain.

There are several other American aircraft crash sites in South Wales, including a P-38 which was on a training flight from Andover, a Marauder on a hilltop near St Davids, and a US Navy Liberator close to the lonely Glyntawe/Trecastle road. It was on a routine night familiarisation flight from Dunkeswell in Devon and all seven

crew were killed. An attack against targets in North-West France on 16 September 1943 resulted in the loss of two B-17s and their crews in the Welsh Mountains. 'Ascend Charlie' was hit in number one engine by flak but maintained formation until the returning aircraft were forced to scatter when they encountered a weather front in gathering darkness. The damaged aircraft failed to clear the mountains near Abergavenny and all ten crew were killed. 'Sondra Kay', an aircraft of the 388th Bomb Group, was lost in similar circumstances.

For much greater detail and background on most of the Mid and South Wales crashes, the reader is recommended to consult *Warplane Wrecks of South Wales and the Marches* by Peter Durham and Dewi Jones.

Parts of the unidentified USAAF F-5 Lightning on Plynlimon bearing underwing codes 'G2-Q'.

AIRSPEED OXFORD

07.01.46	PH242	21 PAFU	Hay Bluff. Engines recovered by 2478 Sqn ATC. Cross-country from Seighford. *161/256358*	S
06.12.53	HM784	63 GPCF	Ebbw Vale Mt. Cardiff. *161/18-06-*	M

AVRO ANSON

17.01.39	L9149	9 E & R FTS	Bannau Brycheiniog. Navex Hamble/Ansty. Memorial plaque in Glyntawe Churchyard. *160/825214*	M
02.03.40	N9879	6 AONS	Black Mts. Navex from Staverton. *161/255354*	S
09.07.40	N5019	15 OTU	Near Llanwrthwl. Navex from Harwell. *148/?*	X
21.09.42	N9745	6 AOS	Near Llanthony. Navex from Staverton. *161/?*	X

AVRO LANCASTER

06.09.43	W4929/ GP-R	1661 HCU	Garn Las. Well scattered. Night navex from Winthorpe. *160/828238*	S

AVRO VULCAN

11.02.66	XH536	Con'sby Wg	Fan Bwlch Chwtyth. Long trail of wreckage. *161/908213*	M

BOEING B-17 FORTRESS

11.04.43	42-29505		Prescelli Mts. Named 'Gunga Din'. Crew survived. *145/?*	X
16.09.43	42-5906	388th BG	Rhiw Gwriadd. Named 'Sondra Kay'. Returning from Bordeaux to Knettishall. *147/01-63-*	S
16.09.43	42-5903	390th BG	Black Mts. Named 'Ascend Charlie'. Returning from Bordeaux with flak damage. Base Framlingham. *161/243253*	

BRISTOL BLENHEIM

22.09.40	L8610	17 OTU	Garn Wen. Navex from Upwood. *161/28-05-*	S

CONSOLIDATED PB4Y-1 LIBERATOR
24.08.44   38753   VB-110 Moel Feity. Night training flight from Dunkeswell.
                                    160/853223   S

CONSOLIDATED B-24 LIBERATOR
19.09.44   EV881   547 Sqn Prescelli Mts. On exercise from St Eval. Memorial on site.
                                    145/128317   S

DE HAVILLAND HORNET
30.09.46   PX273   30 MU Mynydd-y-Glog. On test from St Athan. *160/975094*   M

DE HAVILLAND VAMPIRE
09.10.53   VZ106   233 OCU Bannau Brycheiniog. Pembrey. *160/828204*   L

FAIREY BATTLE
06.10.38   K7589   226 Sqn Plynlimon. Cross-country from Harwell. *135/801871*   S
26.02.40   K7688   9 BGS Prescelli Mts. Cross-country from Penrhos to Stormy Down.
                                    Crew survived. *145/125326*   M

HANDLEY PAGE HALIFAX
12.12.44   LL541   1664 HCU Nant-Yr-Haidd. Mid-air break-up. Dishforth. *147/93-66-*   S

HAWKER HURRICANE
07.01.40   L2074   11 Gp Mynydd William Meyrick. *170/95-92-*   S
29.12.40   W9123   1 FPP 1 mile SSW of Maesteg. Shawbury/St Eval. *170/84-90-*   X
26.09.41   Z3662   79 Sqn Rhigos. Fairwood Common. *170/94-03-*   X

JUNKERS Ju 88
25.04.42   3459/   IV/KG 3 Gwaunceste Hill. Night intruder mission from Brussels-Evere.
              5K+DW   Shot down by Beaufighter X7933 of 25 Sqn. *148/135549*   S

LOCKHEED HUDSON
07.01.40   N7256   233 Sqn Mynydd Maendy. Base was Leuchars. *170/95-89-*   X

LOCKHEED F-5 LIGHTNING
11.09.45   -   7 PG Plynlimon. Training flight from Chalgrove. *136/797870*

LOCKHEED P-38J LIGHTNING
12.04.44   -   402nd FS/ Olchon Valley. Training flight from Andover.
                     370th FG *161/272323*   S

233 OCU Vampire seen at Pembrey, prior to its loss on 9 October 1953.

MARTIN B-26 MARAUDER

04.06.43	41-34765	322nd BG	Carn Lliddi. Ferrying St Mawgan/Valley. *157/73-28-*	S

MILES MARTINET

31.01.44	MS525	7 AGS	3 miles north-east of Port Talbot. Stormy Down. *170/?*	X
21.12.45	HN888	595 Sqn	Near Llandindrod Wells. Found by shepherd 02.02.46. Aberporth/Castle Bromwich.	X

NORTH AMERICAN MUSTANG

07.09.45	KH499	118 Sqn	Mynydd-y-Glog. Fairwood Common. *160/97-09-*	S

SUPERMARINE SPITFIRE

06.08.41	X4381	53 OTU	Near Ton-Pentre. Llandow. *170/?*	S
12.08.41	R7057	53 OTU	Mynydd Pen-y-Cae. Llandow. *170/?*	S
03.11.41	X4913	53 OTU	Pen-y-Fan. Llandow. Wreckage not found until 10.07.42. *161/014215.*	S
03.01.42	P9491	53 OTU	Mynydd-y-Glyn. Llandow. *170/?*	X
08.03.42	L1014	53 OTU	Skirrid Fawr. Spun out of cloud. Llandow. *161/324176*	S
23.05.42	X4588	53 OTU	Brecon Beacons. Wreckage found on 02.06.42. Llandow. *161/017184*	S

VICKERS WELLINGTON

09.12.40	T2520	115 Sqn	Cefn Ystrad. Became lost returning from ops Bordeaux to Marham. *160/088136*	S
06.07.42	R1465/Y	22 OTU	Waen Rydd. Night navex from Wellesborne Mountford. Memorial to all-Canadian crew nearby. *161/062198*	M
26.09.42	BJ697	12 OTU	Black Mt. Navex from Chipping Warden. *160/836182*	S
20.11.44	MF509	22 OTU	Carreg Goch. Night navex from Stratford. Probably iced up in cloud. *161/816171*	L

The author's son Andrew, aged 7, on the wing of Battle K7688 in the Prescelli Hills.

Chapter Thirteen

Dartmoor, Bodmin and Exmoor

Apart from the wrecks on the uplands of South-West England, I have included the three sites on Lundy Island for interest, although they are not strictly high ground incidents. There were few local aerodromes around Dartmoor other than Harrowbeer, which was built for the defence of Plymouth and soon found itself supplying mountain rescue facilities. The group of Coastal Command bases in Cornwall were far enough away from the high ground for it not to have much effect on their operations, but not so the US Navy airfield at Dunkeswell in Devon. The Liberator squadrons of Fleet Air Wing 7 and, in the early days, those of the USAAF's anti-submarine units, were forced to overfly Dartmoor to and from their patrol areas in the Bay of Biscay and the South-West Approaches.

Training aircraft were relatively uncommon over this part of the country, a fact which is readily apparent from a study of the listing. One which did crash was the Spitfire on Brent Moor which in the 'fifties was visible from the air and recognisable. Unfortunately, for this reason it was subsequently buried. Large portions of a Battle, presumably the one at Two Bridges, were recovered by the RAF in 1964 but it is not known what became of them.

Another mystery is that of the USAAF fighter found near Princetown on 2 March 1943 where it had crashed the day before. The 8th Air Force was not active on that particular date, so perhaps it was on a training flight. At that stage of the war it was probably a Thunderbolt. On 22 November 1945, a Vengeance target-tug took off from Exeter for a thirty minute test flight. Neither it nor its pilot were ever seen again. If it did not crash in the Channel, it could have plunged into a Dartmoor bog.

Most of the US Navy Liberator on Steeperton Tor was removed by an RAF salvage unit in a wintertime job which took nine days. Another of their subjects was a burnt-out Skymaster, 42-72249, which had crashed on the moors near Launceston in 1944 whilst inbound to the Trans-atlantic Terminal at St Mawgan. It was reasonably accessible and was removed with the aid of a sledge and tractor.

Dartmoor was ideally placed to catch stray aircraft returning from raids over North-West France. Two Hampdens from Scampton in Lincolnshire were lost in this way within a fortnight on Hamel Down Tor and Hangingstone Hill. The Lancaster on Standon Hill, was however, on a training flight, No. 207 Squadron having just re-equipped with the type.

Close to Hamel Down Tor, on Manaton Hill, is a six foot standing stone which was erected by two local men. On it are engraved the date and initials of five British airmen who were killed in a crash here in 1941. I am not aware of the exact date so cannot verify the aircraft involved. The smooth-heathery hilltop site still has tall wooden posts as a wartime deterrent to enemy aircraft landings.

The Beaufighter in the same area had been on a night patrol from Exeter and evidently descended too soon through cloud. The wreck was salvaged by No. 67 MU and one of the former team members tells me that they lost a wheel and a tyre which disappeared into the undergrowth when they deliberately rolled it downhill to save carrying it! Perhaps it lies there still.

Finally, a word of warning. Whilst watching anxiously for spectral hounds you could just wander into one of the infamous morasses. On a more serious note, vast tracts of the Moor are used as an artillery range, some of the wrecks lying within its boundaries. Local enquiry and warning notices will establish when and where it is safe to go. Suspicious objects should given a wide berth, a precaution also to be observed at many crash sites in this book.

Tailplane of B-24D Liberator 42-40474 which crashed on Hamel Down Tor on 27 December 1943 *(R. Hill)*

ARMSTRONG WHITWORTH WHITLEY

01.06.42	AD698	77 Sqn	Lundy. Returning to Chivenor from patrol. *180/?*	S

AVRO ANSON

28.11.39	N5084	148 Sqn	Exmoor. Cross-country from Harwell. *164/?*	X
28.03.41	L9150	3 OTU	Halfinger Down. Navex from Chivenor. *191/?*	X

AVRO LANCASTER

27.05.42	R5617	207 Sqn	Standon Hill. Cross-country from Bottesford. *191/56-81-*	X

BRISTOL BEAUFIGHTER

27.09.41	R2442	307 Sqn	Hameldon Tor. On patrol from Exeter. *191/70-80-*	X
03.09.45	RD558	151 RU(A)	Withypool. Belgian crew killed. *164/82-35-*	X

BRISTOL BLENHEIM

11.06.41	V5933	53 Sqn	Bodmin Moor. St Eval. *202/?*	X

CONSOLIDATED B-24 LIBERATOR

27.12.43	42-40474	36th BS/ 482nd BG	Hameldon. Training flight from Alconbury. *191/70-80-*	X

CONSOLIDATED PB4Y-1 LIBERATOR

| 03.12.43 | 32014/G | VB-103 | Steeperton Tor. Mostly cleared. Training flight from Dunkeswell. *191/62-89-* | S |
| 28.12.43 | 63926/E | VB-110 | Okehampton Moor. Anti-shipping strike from Dunkeswell. *191/?* | X |

DE HAVILLAND SEA VIXEN

| 31.05.65 | XN648 | 766 Sqn | Near Cranmere Pool. Yeovilton. *191/59-85-* | X |

DE HAVILLAND VAMPIRE

| 25.09.52 | VZ813 | 229 OCU | Dartmoor. Chivenor. *191/?* | S |

DOUGLAS C-47 SKYTRAIN

| 13.10.45 | - | USAAF | Huntingdon Warren. *202/66-67-* | X |

FAIREY BATTLE

| 04.07.39 | K9391 | 150 Sqn | Two Bridges. Cross-country from Benson. *202/?* | X |

FAIREY FULMAR

| 18.01.42 | - | | Tanners Hill, Dartmoor. *191/?* | X |

GLOSTER GLADIATOR

| 20.11.40 | N5644 | 247 Sqn | Near Okehampton. On patrol from St Eval. *191/?* | X |

GLOSTER METEOR

| 14.10.49 | VW434 | 56 Sqn | Near Withypool, Dartmoor. Thorney Island. *191/?* | X |

HANDLEY PAGE HAMPDEN

| 21.03.41 | X3054 | 49 Sqn | Hameldon Tor. Returning to Scampton from ops. *191/70-80-* | X |
| 04.04.41 | AD748 | 83 Sqn | Hangingstone Hill. Returning to Scampton from mine-laying at La Rochelle. *191/61-86-* | X |

HAWKER HUNTER

| 19.03.71 | XG131 | 229 OCU | Near Hawkridge. Chivenor. *164/?* | X |

HEINKEL He 111H-5

| 03.03.41 | 3911/ IG+AL | I/KG27 | Lundy. From Tours. *180/?* | M |
| 01.04.41 | 3837/ IG+FL | I/KG27 | Lundy. From Tours. *180/?* | S |

SHORT STIRLING

| 22.08.42 | R9329/V | 149 Sqn | Near Cornwood. Returning to Lakenheath after mining off French Coast. *202/?* | X |

SUPERMARINE SEAFIRE

| 15.03.48 | SX237 | 736 Sqn | Bodmin Moor. St Merryn. *202/?* | X |

SUPERMARINE SPITFIRE

29.11.41	W3968	317 Sqn	Near Princetown. Patrol from Exeter.	X
16.08.42	P9468	53 OTU	3 miles north of Widdicombe. Lost, pilot baled out. Llandow. *202/?*	X
06.12.42	EP749	19 Sqn	White Tor. Perranporth. *191/54-79-*	X
23.10.47	TE406	203 AFS	Brent Moor. Mainly buried. Chivenor. *202/654640*	S

VICKERS WELLINGTON

| 06.10.42 | BX281 | 142 Sqn | Near Princetown. On ops from Waltham | X |
| 01.03.44 | LN775 | 3 OADU | Two Barrows, Dartmoor. Ferrying overseas. | X |

Chapter Fourteen

Northern Ireland

The crash sites in the Province reflect the wide variety of operational and training types based there during the Second World War. Thanks are due to Ernie Cromie of the Ulster Aviation Society for expanding considerably the lists in previous editions. One location not yet traced, however, is where a USAAF Liberator from Cluntoe crashed on 2 March 1944.

There were twenty active airfields during the last war as well as the flying boat bases at Castle Archdale and Killadeas on Lough Erne. Coastal Command flew from Aldergrove, Nutts Corner, Ballykelly and Limavady and there were fighter stations at Ballyhalbert and Kirkistown. The USAAF occupied several airfields in a training and support role, Langford Lodge, Cluntoe and Toome being the most important. There was also a Coastal OTU at Long Kesh, a navigation school at Bishops Court and Royal Naval Air Stations at Eglinton and Maydown.

With all this flying going on it is not surprising that there were so many accidents on the extensive high ground to be found over much of the region. One notorious example is the mountain known as Benevenagh which was close to the aerodromes along the coastal strip bordering Lough Foyle, dangerously so in the case of Limavady where it rises within the circuit area. It proved fatal to many and Shackleton crews of a later era nicknamed it 'Ben Twitch'.

The hills around Belfast saw many crashes but it is believed that virtually all wreckage was removed because they are fairly easy to reach. There is certainly evidence of some of them, however, and all known accidents on this high ground have been included for information. The B-17 on Cave Hill was on the final stage of a Transatlantic ferry flight and there were several other losses of British aircraft flying to and from Nutts Corner.

The Coastal OTU at Long Kesh, now the site of The Maze Prison, operated many Beauforts, a few of which flew into hills. The two Mosquitoes from High Ercall in Shropshire were engaged in practice night intruding over Ulster airfields. This was a standard exercise on the curriculum as the Irish Sea crossing could simulate the English Channel. The two Beaufighters lost during 1942 were operational aircraft on night patrols from Ballyhalbert.

The transport aircraft involved in a crash near Maghera in September 1943 is now known to have been a Cessna Bobcat and the commander of the US Navy base at Londonderry was one of the fatal casualties. There were two survivors from the crew of another American aircraft, a Fortress, which came down near Cushendall in 1942. At least two Marauders from the 3rd Combat Crew Replacement Centre at Toome were wrecked in high ground accidents. This unit gave brief familiarisation in British weather conditions and flying procedures to crews newly arrived from the USA for the 9th Air Force.

As well as the Sunderland on Knocklayd Mountain, there was almost another Sunderland loss in the Province when an aircraft of No.423 Squadron struck a hilltop, severely damaging the hull and leaving pieces which were later removed by No.226 MU. The flying boat subsequently crash-landed at Jurby aerodrome on the Isle of Man and caught fire. Widespread damage was caused when the depth charges eventually went off.

Navigational exercises were flown constantly over Northern Ireland, often at night, from local airfields and those observer schools on the mainland and the Isle of Man. At least six Ansons were lost in the hills in various parts of Ulster during the war years. The solitary Oxford was a squadron 'hack' based at Ballykelly, local people playing an important part in bringing help for the injured crew in appalling weather conditions.

AIRSPEED OXFORD

15.12.44	AS874	59 Sqn	Coolcosreaghan. Ballykelly. *H/79-09-*	x

AVRO ANSON

31.01.40	N4943	1 AONS	Near Cushendall. Navex from Prestwick.	X
09.11.42	AX322	1 AOS	4½ miles north-west of Moneymore. Navex from Wigtown.	X
18.12.42	DJ572	5 AOS	5 miles north-west of Moneymore. Navex from Jurby.	X
23.02.43	EG460	1 OAFU	Brackaghslievegallion. Navex from Wigstown.	X
21.04.44	N5168	7 OAFU	Near Cushendall. Navex from Bishops Court.	X
06.03.45	LV153	1 OAFU	Mullaghclogha. Navex from Wigtown.	S
07.07.47	NK877	2 ANS	Meenard Mt. Navex from Bishops Court. *H/661980*	S

BOEING B-17 FORTRESS

03.10.42	41-24451	91st BG	Near Cushendall. Two survived. Gander/Prestwick.	X
01.06.44	'7862'		Cave Hill. Ferrying Gander/Nutts Corner. *J/32-80-*	X

BRISTOL BEAUFIGHTER

26.05.42	X7573	153 Sqn	Near Moneyreagh. Loss of control in cloud. Ballyhalbert.	X
19.07.42	X7822	153 Sqn	Mourne Mts. On night patrol from Ballyhalbert. *J/250214*	S

BRISTOL BEAUFORT

20.01.43	L9828	5 OTU	Ballycollin Hill. Operational training from Long Kesh. *J/26-70-*	X
29.03.43	AW277	5 OTU	Collin Mt. Operational training from Long Kesh. *J/26-70-*	X
17.06.43	JM452	5 OTU	Divis Mt. Operational training from Long Kesh. *J/280753*	S
23.07.43	JM451/18	5 OTU	5 miles west of Swatragh, Antrim. Operational training from Long Kesh.	X

CESSNA UC-78 BOBCAT

04.09.43		USAAF	Near Maghera. C-in-C US Navy base Londonderry killed. Eglinton/Hendon.	X

CONSOLIDATED CATALINA

20.11.44	JX242/P	202 Sqn	Magho Hill, Fermanagh. On anti-sub patrol from Castle Archdale.	X

CONSOLIDATED B-24 LIBERATOR

04.05.42	AL558/B	120 Sqn	Divis Mt. Nutts Corner. *J/270754*	S
26.08.42	LV340	120 Sqn	Antrim. In bad weather Ballykelly/Nutts Corner.	X
03.11.42	AL519	120 Sqn	Benevenagh. On night flying practice from Ballykelly.	X
24.06.44	FL977/H.	59 Sqn	Benevenagh. On approach to Ballykelly.	X
30.01.45	EW628	1332 HCU	Standing Stones Hill. Navex from Nutts Corner. *J/25-74-*	X
16.02.45	EV954	1674 HCU	Collindale. Antrim. Navex from Aldergrove.	X
19.03.45	KG896	1674 HCU	Tornagrough, Antrim. Operational training from Aldergrove. *J/25-73-*	X

DE HAVILLAND DOMINIE

15.09.53	NF861/LP-002	703 Sqn	Glendun Mt. Stretton/Eglinton.	X

DE HAVILLAND HORNET MOTH

31.07.41	W9380	24 Sqn	Sperrin Mts. Reconnoitring AA guns in Londonderry area.	S

DE HAVILLAND MOSQUITO

14.03.44	DZ718	60 OTU	3 miles east of Dromore. Intruder exercise from High Ercall. *J/307505*	S
13.01.45	NS996	60 OTU	Slieve Commedagh. Intruder exercise from High Ercall. *J/349279*	M

FAIREY BATTLE

22.10.40	P6601	226 Sqn	Trostan. Operational patrol from Sydenham.	M

LOCKHEED HUDSON

16.08.41	AM588	206 Sqn	4 miles north-east of Ladyhill, Antrim. Night flying from Aldergrove.	X
12.04.42	V9112	1527 BATF	Crockaneel Mt. From Prestwick	S

MARTIN B-26 MARAUDER

10.04.44		3 CCRC	Mourne Mts. Lost formation during practice flight from Toome.	S
21.06.44		3 CCRC	Slieve Gallion. Believed cleared. Three survived. Toome.	

SHORT SUNDERLAND

05.12.43	W6013	423 Sqn	Knocklayd Mt, Ballycastle. Descended too early through cloud. Castle Archdale.	X

SUPERMARINE SEAFIRE

02.10.45	SR482	803 Sqn	Slievenanee. Nutts Corner. *D/160218*	S

SUPERMARINE SPITFIRE

17.02.43	AB960	501 Sqn	Slieve Greeba. On night cross-country from Ballyhalbert.	X

VICKERS WELLINGTON

16.03.42	X3599	57 Sqn	Thomas Mt. Engines recovered by Ulster Aviation Society in 1984. Feltwell/Aldergrove. *J/363293*	S
02.01.43	W5713	7 OTU	Binevenagh. In blizzard. Crew survived. Limavady.	X
13.07.43	HF838	7 OTU	Binevenagh. In the circuit for Limavady.	X
12.09.43	X9820	105 OTU	Slieve Commedagh. On navex from Bramcote. *J/343286*	S
17.09.43	W5647	7 OTU	Scawt Hill, Antrim. Navex from Limavady. One fatal casualty. *J/33-09-*	X
05.11.43	LB247	7 OTU	Binevenagh. In Limavady. Circuit in bad weather. One fatal casualty.	X
24.11.43	Z1313	104 OTU	Divis Mt. On instrument approach to Nutts Corner. *J/28-75-*	X
31.12.43	T1520	104 OTU	Rushey Hill, Dunrod. Returning to Nutts Corner from navex. *J/24-72-*	X

WESTLAND LYSANDER

17.03.43	P9125	1 APC	White Abbey, Antrim. Aldergrove.	X

Opposite, top: **One of the engines of Wellington X3599 on Thomas Mt, before recovery by the Ulster Aviation Society in 1984** (*E. A. Cromie*)

Opposite bottom: **Illustrating the Irish Republic section is this engine from Sunderland DD848 on Mt Brandon** (*G. O'Regan*)

Chapter Fifteen

Irish Republic

Although of course neutral during the Second World War, Eire was overflown frequently, unintentionally or otherwise, by Allied and German aircraft. The mountain ranges along the south and west coasts claimed some of them and so many crashed on Mount Brandon in County Kerry that the British requested a geological survey. It was suspected that mineral deposits were affecting aircraft compasses but no evidence was found to support this theory, nor for the more sinister one that a German agent had placed a decoy radio beacon on the mountain! It seems the real reason was that the high ground was on a long peninsula projecting into the Atlantic.

Most of the British losses were Coastal Command aircraft from bases in Northern Ireland, the mountains of Donegal being a particular hazard to those straying over neutral territory in bad weather. No. 59 Squadron from Ballykelly lost two Liberators here in a single night soon after take-off when both failed to clear the high ground. They were loaded with fuel and depth charges and all sixteen crew were killed. The Blue Stack Mountains claimed a Sunderland from Pembroke Dock in January 1944 while it was diverting to Lough Erne after an anti-submarine patrol. Local people have painted a simple memorial inscription to the crew on a rock close to the crash site.

Still in Donegal, a Hampden which was returning to base in Lincolnshire after a raid on Germany became hopelessly lost and eventually collided with the Glendowan Mountains. During March 1945, a Sunderland hit a hill near Killybegs just prior to setting course on a U-boat patrol, killing all twelve on board. North-west Eire was the scene of another Coastal Command accident after the war when a Halifax on a weather sortie came down on Achill Island.

As mentioned above, Brandon Mountain was the downfall of four aircraft. The earliest was a Focke-Wulf Condor in August 1940 which was on a routine long range armed reconnaissance from Bordeaux to Norway. The pilot must have seen the ground at the last moment, pulled the stick back and stalled onto a steep slope. Incredibly only two of the crew were slightly hurt and the wreck was set on fire in customary fashion. Because this was the first German aircraft to crash in Ireland, the military authorities removed much of the wreckage, including three of the engines, for investigation. The site is still well worth a visit however, and a local farmer has adapted pieces as gates and parts of walls, the Luftwaffe camouflage being discernible.

Two Sunderlands crashed on Brandon within a month, the RAF flying boat being on an Atlantic patrol, while the BOAC example was operating the Lisbon-Foynes leg of the company's West Africa service. It was carrying the first POW mail from Japan and local people painstakingly collected all the scattered letters for onward delivery. Unexploded depth charges could be seen at the RAF Sunderland site until quite recently when the Irish Army finally decided to deal with them! The Wellington nearby had an all-Polish crew, none of whom survived.

There was once an intriguing rumour that the remains of a Junkers 52 lay near the Gap of Dunloe in Kerry. It was supposed to have been lost dropping German agents into Eire but the story may have been confused with the French-built Ju 52 which crashed in the Wicklow Mountains in 1946. The French Air Force aircraft was flying a party of girl guides to Dublin when in hit high ground, coming to rest virtually intact with no fatalities. It was not salvaged but the ubiquitous tinkers removed it piecemeal and there is said to be nothing left today.

Late in the war, RAF salvage teams were allowed almost free access to the Republic to recover wreckage and much of what they abandoned was subsequently cleared by the tinkers for its scrap value. The reputedly large remains of a Catalina on Stradbally Mountain were removed quite recently by a local farmer when his sheep suffered from the effects of chewing on lead-covered wiring!

Irish aviation enthusiasts have placed memorials at a number of crash sites in the south of the country, including the Liberator in the Caha Mountains. Another commemorates the crew of a USAAF C-47 which crashed on one of Ireland's highest peaks in a particular rugged and remote area.

The recovered tailwheel from the Focke-Wulf Fw 200 Condor on Mt Brandon.

CESSNA 182

19.11.68	5Y-AIN		Slieve Felim, Limerick. Bembridge/Shannon.	X
07.09.85	G-BKGY		Blackstairs Mt. Birmingham/Kilkenny.	X

CESSNA 185A

29.06.67	EI-AMT		Lugnaquilla, Co Wicklow.	M

CONSOLIDATED CATALINA

21.01.41	AM265	240 Sqn	Glengad Mt. Leitrim. Patrol from Loch Erne.	X
19.12.44	JX208/F	202 Sqn	Stradbally Mt. On anti-sub patrol from Castle Archdale.	S

CONSOLIDATED B-24 LIBERATOR

16.03.42	AL577/N	108 Sqn	Slieve Na Glogh. North Africa/Southern England. Radio unserviceable. Completely lost.	X
27.08.43	BZ802/V	86 Sqn	Caha Mt. Returning to Ballykelly from anti-sub patrol.	M
19.06.44	FL990/A	59 Sqn	Donegal. Anti-sub patrol in bad weather from Ballykelly.	X
19.06.44	FL989/L	59 Sqn	Glengad Head, Donegal. Soon after take-off from Ballykelly on anti-sub patrol.	X

DOUGLAS C-47 SKYTRAIN

17.12.43	43-30719	437th TCG	Cummeenapeasta, Kerry. Ferrying Port Lyautey/St Mawgan. Memorial nearby.	S

FOCKE-WULF Fw 200 CONDOR
20.08.40   III/KG40 Mt Brandon. Operational flight Bordeaux/Norway. Crew all
                                  survived.   M

HANDLEY PAGE HALIFAX
16.06.50 RG843/Y3-O 202 Sqn Croaghaun, Achill Island. Met sortie from Aldergrove.   M

HANDLEY PAGE HAMPDEN
02.10.41 AD768   106 Sqn Glendowan Mts. Donegal. Became lost returning to Coningsby
                                from ops to Karlsruhe.   X

JUNKERS Ju 52 (AAC-1)
12.08.46 No.46/B   FAF Wicklow Mts. All 28 on board survived. Le Bourget/Dublin.   X

JUNKERS Ju 88
03.03.42 1429/CN+OU Wek 2 Mt Gabriel, Co Cork. Weather reconnaissance flight from
                              North-west France.   S

LOCKHEED HUDSON
11.01.41 N7298   224 Sqn Kildare. On patrol from Leuchars.   X
27.09.41 AE577   ATFERO Near Dundalk. Baldonnel/Prestwick.   X

SHORT SUNDERLAND
29.07.43 G-AGES   BOAC Mt Brandon. Lisbon/Foynes   S
22.08.43 DD848/N   201 Sqn Mt Brandon. Anti-sub patrol from Castle Archdale.   M
31.01.44 DW110   228 Sqn Bluestack Mts. Donegal.   M
14.03.45 ML743/ZM-A 201 Sqn Near Killybegs. Outbound on patrol from Castle Archdale.   M

SUPERMARINE SEAFIRE
28.05.51 154   IAC Carrie Hill, Wicklow Mts. Training flight from Gormanston.   X

VICKERS VESPA
18.05.31 V3   IAC Foxford Mts. Mayo   X

VICKERS WELLINGTON
11.04.41 W5653   221 Sqn Fort Dunrae, Donegal. Anti-sub patrol from Limavady.   X
20.12.43 HF208   304 Sqn Mt Brandon. On anti-submarine patrol from Predannack.   M

Opposite top: **The memorial to the C-47 crew killed on Cummeenapeasta, Kerry on
17 December 1943** *(G. O'Regan).*

Opposite bottom: **Tail wreckage from Sunderland DW110 in Blue Stack mountains,
Donegal** *(E. A. Cromie)*

DOUGLAS C-47 SKYTRAIN
43-00719
CRASHED NEAR HERE
17 DECEMBER 1943

2ND LT. J.L. SCHARF
2ND LT. L.E. GOODIN
2ND LT. F.V. BROSSARD
S. SGT. W.T. HOLSTLAW
SGT. A.A. SCHWARTZ
LEST WE FORGET

Mountain Rescue

Before the War collisions with high ground were relatively few and could be dealt with by the nearest RAF station with local civilian help. However, with the enormous increase in flying after the outbreak of war the problem soon became acute. For example, in 1942 No.23 Group Flying Training Command who were responsible for the (Pilot) Advanced Flying Units reported that 158 aircrew had been involved in high ground accidents with eighty-six killed and forty-two injured. The training of bomber crews was so urgent to maintain the night offensive against Germany that flights were carried out twenty-four hours a day in all weathers. The result was not surprising; crews got lost on cross-country flights due to inexperience and minimal navigation aids and were faced with an unenviable choice, whether to descend through cloud and risk hitting a hill or to bale out over what might turn out to be the sea. Operational aircraft returning from raids over the Continent also went astray, their difficulties compounded by battle damage, fatigue and bad weather. USAAF aircraft, although based in East Anglia, occasionally flew into mountains on training flights and also a number were lost in transit from the States. The ferry pilots of the Air Transport Auxiliary often came to grief whilst following valleys in deteriorating weather when trying to deliver a badly needed aircraft.

Measures were taken to produce the tragic loss of life, the most important of which was *GRANITE*, the code name given to a Royal Observer Corps operation designed to prevent aircraft flying into hills in poor visibility. When instructed by their parent centre or on their own initiative, ROC posts in hilly districts would light red flares to warn aircraft in the vicinity. In association with *DARKY*, the method of homing aircraft lost or in distress to the nearest suitable aerodrome, the number of high ground collisions was sharply reduced although still very high. Mountain Warning Beacon Transmitters, known officially as 'Squeakers' from the signal they emitted, were placed on many areas of high ground, for example Foel Grach and Cwm Silyn in Snowdonia, Snaefell on the Isle of Man and Black Combe and Coniston Old Man in the Lake District. They were the same as Balloon Squeakers and provided an audible warning of half a second's duration repeated every six seconds if the aircraft had the common frequency of 6440 Khz tuned in. Red hazard lights or, in certain areas, aerial lighthouses called Occult beacons, were placed on hilltops known to be particularly dangerous to aircraft.

The more populated parts of the country were covered by a network of ROC posts which would log the details of passing aircraft and telephone them to the next post on their presumed flight path. If an aircraft failed to appear over the next post or adjacent one, the RAF parent Sector HQ was alerted so that prompt search action could be taken for any aircraft subsequently reported missing. The Mosquito on Corserine in southern Scotland was found in this way, the local observers even predicting where it had impacted. In the more remote areas, ROC posts were thinly spread and early in 1941 the Air Ministry appealed via the newspapers for postmen in hilly districts to keep a look out for crashed aeroplanes on their early morning rounds and report them immediately.

In many cases, however, the first indication of a crash was an exhausted, blood-stained figure knocking on a cottage door in the small hours. Many tales of heroism can be told about crashes in the hills and a number of medals were awarded to injured airmen who struggled for help for their comrades. The gallantry of some civilian and military rescuers was also recognised in this way, usually with a British Empire Medal. Such was the tenacity of the searchers that very few survivors are known to have succumbed to their injuries or exposure before help arrived.

In the early stages of the war, it became apparent that the discovery of a crashed aircraft in the mountains was often a matter of chance and the subsequent removal of casualties a difficult problem. RAF units near mountainous areas would organise their own search parties using the most suitable personnel and equipment available. Servicing of aircraft suffered accordingly while trained airmen were absent on a rescue operation and thus the establishment of a specialised Mountain Rescue Service arose from a need recognised at station level, rather than a directive from Air Ministry.

During April 1942, Flight Lieutenant George Graham, Station Medical Officer at RAF Llandwrog in North Wales, organised a search and rescue party which was later to become the model on which the RAF MRS was to be based. His team consisted mainly of medical orderlies and attendants from the Station Sick Quarters, backed up by a 'search and carry' element comprising airmen of any trade. By the end of the year, these mountain rescuers had brought twelve aircrew to safety and recovered thirty-five bodies from eleven crashes in North and Mid-Wales.

However, shortcomings soon became apparent. An arduous search for an Anson in the Carneddau went on for two and a half days before it was successful. The injured pilot had struggled down to a farm and reported that other crew members were alive but could give no definite

Members of the Mountain Rescue Team at Llandwrog with Humber ambulance in front of Sick Bay. From left, second Cpl G. McTigue, third F/Lt G. Graham, fourth F/O Scudamore. *(Mrs M. McTigue)*

position for the wreck. Communications between the search parties were non-existent apart from Very lights and rations had to be ferried up by local civilian vehicles as no service transport could negotiate the steep mountain tracks. To remedy these faults Flight Lieutenant Graham therefore proposed a unit specially equipped for mountain rescue and, when this proposal had been accepted, he conducted his first mountain rescue trial in the Conway Valley in 1943.

Four months later he declared his unit ready for action. Ropes, maps, compasses and windproof clothing were supplied and portable radios were provided for search parties. A jeep was acquired to carry advance parties quickly into the mountains. By the end of October the unit had attended eight aircraft crashes - including a search lasting two and a half days in Snowdonia.

Since 571 Allied airmen had lost their lives in crashes in the upland areas of the United Kingdom in 1943, the Air Ministry now became convinced that the hitherto *ad hoc* rescue arrangements should be co-ordinated and controlled from a central point and that more assistance - in the form of specialist equipment and training - should be available to volunteers on mountain rescue operations.

During January 1944 the Air Ministry announced that a Mountain Rescue Service had been formed in order to facilitate the search for, and rescue of, aircrews who had crashed in mountainous districts within a radius of forty miles of RAF stations Llandwrog, Millom and Wigtown. The rescue crews available on these stations were specially trained and provided with ambulances, ancillary transport and radio equipment. By the end of the year eight teams were in evidence and had attended fifty-four crashes, rescuing forty-nine aircrew out of the 226 involved. The other units were located at Wick, Montrose and Kinloss in Scotland, Harpur Hill in Derbyshire and Madley in Herefordshire. Some of them had come into being, unofficially, a considerable time before. A further team which never seemed to aspire to official recognition operated from RAF Harrowbeer on the fringes of Dartmoor.

Many RAF stations closed at the end of the war, causing the Wigtown team to move to West Freugh, the Llandwrog team to Llanbedr, and the Montrose to Dyce. As flying resumed its peacetime level, several of the units disbanded but much was done to improve the service during the ensuing decade. More sophisticated equipment was provided and training courses in rock climbing, winter mountaineering and rescue were introduced for potential team leaders and members. Later, RAF Mountain Rescue was expanded to cover overseas areas with the formation of teams in Cyprus (1954), Aden (1960) and Hong Kong (1961). Currently active in the UK are teams at Kinloss, Leuchars, St Athan and Stafford.

The MU Salvage Parties

With the outbreak of the Second World War the expansion of aerial activity resulted in an enormous increase in accidents. Many of the aircraft could be repaired and put back into service and the write-offs could be stripped of useful parts and melted down as valuable scrap. The small peacetime organisation for salvage was obviously inadequate and on 19 September 1939 six separate Salvage Centres were formed. Two weeks later, it was decided by Air Ministry that in the interests of security the term 'Salvage Centre' should be discontinued and the centres would be redesignated as Maintenance Units and numbered within the normal system for these units. The six original units were soon reinforced by several more so that the whole of the UK could be covered.

Those MU's whose area encompassed mountainous country were as follows:—

No.34 Shrewsbury, Shropshire
No.56 Inverness
No.60 Leconfield, Yorkshire
No.63 Carluke, Lanarkshire
No.67 Taunton, Somerset
No.75 Wilmslow, Cheshire
No.78 Bynea, South Wales
No.83 Woolsington, Newcastle-on-Tyne
No.226 Mullusk, Northern Ireland

Each MU had a dozen or more salvage gangs who operated independently, with the result that standards varied widely. Sometimes, aircraft that had crashed quite close to a road were hardly touched and others, virtually inaccessible, were totally removed. All sorts of vehicles were used, including bren gun carriers, tractors, Cletracs and horse-drawn sledges. From

May 1943 it was officially agreed that the RAF would be responsible for salvaging USAAF aircraft in Britain with American help when requested.

Another reason for clearing a crashed aircraft was that it would be reported again and again as a new crash by over-flying aircraft. This happened in Snowdonia in 1944 when a Boston which had crashed two years before was reported by an Anson and the Mountain Rescue Unit had to turn out to check it. An unprecedented effort was made on St Kilda with Sunderland ML858. The salvage gang dug thirty-seven holes 8 x 8 x 4 feet deep to bury the smaller wreckage. The larger hull parts were inverted, weighted with stones and covered with peat. Any bare metal showing was painted brown to camouflage it from the air and prevent further reports of a crash. In other inaccessible areas the remains were buried but often the peat has dried out and the metal has become exposed.

There was also the question of the disfiguring of beautiful areas with large chunks of aeroplane. One would have thought that the environment was disregarded in wartime, but great clearance efforts were made, for example, in the Lake District. The B-17 on Skiddaw was sledged down the mountain in sections and this was done with many others in the Lakes. Fabric covered aircraft like the Anson and Oxford were simply set on fire and the remains chopped up and buried in the spot. There is a curious lack of consistency with the salvage operations.

No.56 MU probably had the toughest job as their area included most of the Scottish Highlands. One of their difficult recoveries was Whitley LA837 on the Hills of Cromdale. The wreck was lying in a peat bog at about 2,000 ft and the wintry conditions made it impossible to approach the site with either a tractor or horse. Vehicles could not be brought beyond the point of three miles away at the foot of the mountain and the site was eventually cleared by manpower alone.

No.63 MU undertook a particularly gruelling task early in 1944 after a Liberator crashed on a hill near Loch Maddie on the island of North Uist. The salvage party dismantled the aircraft and manhandled it to the beach over difficult country. There was no road by which to take the salvaged portions and engines around the loch and no boat available to carry them across. A raft was improvised from telegraph poles and four 50-gallon drums. The weather was so bad that on only one day in five was it calm enough to ferry the raft across. Salvage operations extended over a period of four months but during prolonged periods of bad weather, a Fortress aircraft was also salvaged.

No.83 MU's area consisted of the Scottish Border and most of the Lake District. A typical salvage job was the removal of the B-17 from the 3,000 ft summit of Skiddaw which was rendered even more difficult by steep slopes covered with scree. All components of this aircraft were manhandled to the foot of the mountain and then transported by means of sledge and tractor to the nearest approach road.

No.60 MU was responsible for the Yorkshire Moors and parts of the Peak District and one of their harder operations was the recovery of Oxford LX518 from the Moors near Penistone. All the salvageable parts, including the engines, had to be sledged one and a half miles across rough country to the loading point, the whole job taking nine days.

No.75 MU tackled a few crashes on the Lancashire Fells, notably Spitfire AD230 on White Moss Fell. Most of the aeroplane was removed on sledges towed by tractors, during a three-week period.

Nos.34 and 78 MUs covered North and South Wales, respectively, but neither recorded its activities in detail which is a pity considering what must have been achieved.

The Dartmoor area was handled by No.67 MU and during December 1943 they salvaged four US Navy PB4Y Liberators. One of them on Steeperton Tor presented considerable difficulties until a US Army detachment at Okehampton Camp loaned them a six-wheel drive vehicle. One stream had to be bridged with railway sleepers and another had its bed built up with rocks to enable the vehicles to cross. The operation employed fifteen men and took nine days to accomplish.

No.226 MU carried out many jobs in Northern Ireland but why did they take so much trouble to remove Anson MG478 from Slieve Croob when a Mosquito in the Mountains of Mourne was declared impossible to salvage and simply dumped in a convenient ravine? They took twenty-two days to recover the Anson, even dismantling the engines and carrying them piece by piece to the nearest road. The airframe was cut up and dragged to the loading point.

The salvage units considered themselves the forgotten men of the RAF, fighting the rain and the mud to put aircraft back into the air or to provide the raw material for new ones. Modern crash sites, especially the military ones, tend to be cleared promptly with the aid of a helicopter. However, such is the fragmentation associated with high-speed jet accidents, much is overlooked....

Component Numbers

An aircraft is a very complex piece of machinery and most . components are marked with a number and an inspector's stamp. The numbers are a necessity for stores identification and for ordering parts in service. Obviously, they can be very complicated and one would need a parts catalogue to identify a particular part by its number. However, if only a few pieces are found at an unidentified crash-site, a component number can identify the manufacturer, sometimes the specific type and, occasionally, even the mark number.

The part number sequences commonly relate to the type number allocated to a particular aircraft during its initial design stage. For example, what was to become the Spitfire was submitted to the Air Ministry as the Supermarine Type 300. Subsequent marks each had a type number, such as 329 for a mk.II and 349 for a mk.V, but basic components common to all Spitfires retained the original 300 prefix.

Some American manufacturers followed a similar system, examples being 32 for the Liberator (Consolidated Model 32) and 22 for the Lightning (Lockheed Model 322). Marauder component numbers, in contrast, appear to have begun 266, which bears no resemblance to its Martin Model number 179. Clearly there were no hard and fast rules.

German aircraft followed a logical system which is too complex to detail here. Suffice it to say that the aircraft type number was incorporated as in the prefix 8-109E (airframe Bf 109E) which would be followed by further groups of numbers to identify the component.

Shortly after the First World War the Aeronautical Inspection Directorate (AID) was established to ensure that all British aircraft, military and civil, were inspected at every stage of production. Each qualified inspector had a stamp by which he could be identified, e.g. AID 216. In addition to government-employed inspectors, certain approved firms making aircraft and parts employed their own inspectors who held AID approval. These inspectors used stamps which either bore the initials of their firm or some two or three letter code.

Unfortunately, there is scope for confusion here, as aircraft types designed by one manufacturer were not necessarily built by him but often sub-contracted to another firm. Examples of this are the Lancasters built by Armstrong Whitworth and Vickers, Walrus by Saunders Roe, Swordfish and Sunderlands by Blackburn, Typhoons and Hurricanes by Gloster, Hampdens and Halifaxes by English Electric and Spitfires by Westland.

The letters AGS can be found on many standard items fitted to British aircraft, such as pipe connectors and locking plates. They stand for Aircraft General Standard and obviously give no clue to the type of aircraft. The Air Ministry also devised a system of standard assemblies which could be fitted to many different types of service aircraft. Each was identified by an 'AM' stamp and a number relating only to the type of equipment, not the type of aircraft. A few examples are:

AM Ref No. 5   Electrical equipment
AM Ref No. 6   Navigational and optical equipment
AM Ref No. 14 Photographic equipment

Most American-built aircraft had all kinds of inscriptions stamped on the inside of the alloy skinning, which have nothing to do with the type. A Fortress inside fuselage, for example, had words like ALCLAD (trade name for alloy), ALCOA (Aluminium Corporation of America) and ANA-04" (the metal's gauge or thickness), stamped at regular intervals. Post-war jet aircraft usually have their part numbers stencilled on in indelible ink or paint, rather than stamped into the metal. This is to prevent stress cracks forming around weak points, such as imprinted numbers.

Inspectors Stamps

AS	Airspeed
AW	Armstrong Whitworth
R3	Avro
BP	Boulton Paul
DH	De Havilland
EEP	English Electric, Preston
F8	Fairey
HP	Handley Page
PPA	Miles (Phillips & Powis)
R	Republic
SFR	Rootes, Speke
SR	Saunders Roe
TAY	Taylorcraft
VA	Vickers Armstrong
	(VACB = Castle Bromwich)
	(VACH = Chester)
	(VABL = Blackpool)
WA	Westland

Component Number Prefixes

SB	Short Bros	G5	Gloster
41H	Hawker	98	Mosquito
NA73	Mustang	SP	Whitley
22	Lightning	32	Liberator
285	Wellington	300	Spitfire
52	Hampden	57	Halifax
FB	Bristol	10	Oxford
20	Commando	62	Mitchell
66	Harvard		

The above are, of course, only brief notes on this complicated subject and research is still in progress to determine other manufacturers' numbering systems.

However, as examples of the complexity, and for their own intrinsic interest, more detailed notes on the Halifax and Mosquito follow.

HALIFAX PART NUMBERING

Mk.I	all part nos start with 57 (derived from H.P.57)
Mk.II	some part nos start with 59
Mk.III	some part nos start with 61
Mk.VI	some part nos start with 61
Mk.VII	some part nos start with 61
Mk.V	some part nos start with 63

NB: These are generalisations - various discrepancies are noted below.

Sometimes 60 is used on fuselage parts. Nearly all aircraft carry 57 as the basic airframe number, only changes in airframe, engines etc appertaining to the different marks carry numbers 59, 61 and 63.

Within each set of numbers is a letter signifying as follows:

A Layout and charts
B Wings, ailerons and flaps
C Fuselage structure
D Undercarriage and hydraulics
E Flying controls, automatic and manual
F Tailplane, fin, rudder and elevators
H Power plant, tanks, piping and engine controls
L Electrical and general equipment
P Ancillary (ground) equipment
Q Armament
R Repairs
S Small standards
T to W Temporary drawings related to B to Q
X Rubber sections
Y Extrusions
Z and ZH Drawn sections

Let us take for example the part number '57193E-2', the breakdown of number and letters being as follows:

=	
57	for Mk.I aircraft
193	drawing number
E	for flying controls
2	for starboard
	Odd numbers = Port
	Even numbers = Starboard

A Mk.II aircraft would be marked 57 except for engines, undercarriage and other small alterations to the basic airframe. This would also apply to Mks.III, V, VI and VII.

As the Halifax was constructed by a number of different companies, a variety of different factory inspectors' stamps are likely to be encountered. A typical example, i.e. EEP in a circle for 'English Electric, Preston'. Rootes-built aircraft often carried the company name in full stencilled on many parts of the airframe.

The above details are intended as a guide to the identification of wreckage where there is doubt as to the type of aircraft involved. Apart from the standard position just forward of and below the tailplane, the RAF serial number is often marked unofficially on the insides of removeable parts such as cowlings, inspection panels, hatches etc. This was done to avoid confusion during servicing and obviously followed no set pattern. Sometimes only the last 'three' were used, e.g. '286 PO' for 'LW286 Port Outer'. Any airframe fitter will tell you that seemingly identical panels from different aircraft of the same type will often refuse to fit if transposed!

MOSQUITO PART NUMBERING

The part number consists of the following:
   a 'unit code' letter — see below
   an 'Aircraft type' identification - (always 98 for the Mosquito)
   a part number serial (within each 'Unit code')
Odd part numbers identify an 'as drawn' (generally left hand part), whilst the next consecutive even number would be its complementary 'opposite hand' part. Unit code letters were as follows:
A, B, C Fuselage
D, E, F Wings
      G Undercarriage
      J Tail Unit
      K Flying controls
      L Engine installation
      N Electrics
      P Fuel
      Q Hydraulics
      R Radio
      S Services
      Z Miscellaneous
Examples: A984131 indicates Part no. 4131 (left side or as drawn) of a Mosquito fuselage. A984132 indicates the 'opposite hand' version of A984131.

Country Code

1. Guard against all risk of fire.

2. Fasten all gates.

3. Keep dogs under proper control.

4. Leave no litter.

5. Keep to the paths across farmland.

6. Avoid damaging fences, hedges and walls.

7. Safeguard water supplies.

8. Protect wild life, wild plants and trees.

9. Go carefully on country roads.

10. Respect the life of the countryside.

Mountain Code

1. Plan, with maps.

2. Don't try too much too soon. Move gradually to bigger things.

3. Go with others and keep together always. Until experienced don't take charge of others: then take only ten or less.

4. Equip against the worst. Be well shod: have warm clothing and a waterproof cover, spare clothes and food for all, map, whistle, torch and compass.

5. Give yourself ample time, and more as a reserve. Move steadily. Don't hurry and don't waste time.

6. Don't throw down or dislodge rocks or stones. Know and observe the Country Code.

7. Eye the weather: it can change completely in a few hours. Don't go on recklessly if it turns bad. Don't be afraid to come down.

8. Don't go rock, snow or ice climbing without an experienced leader.

9. If lost don't panic or rush down. Keep together and deliberately work out your position and your best way down.

10. Leave word behind you of your route and when you expect to be back. If you arrive where friends don't expect you, 'phone them or tell the police (to save needless searches).

Bibliography

Aircraft Down, Air Crashes in Wharfedale and Nidderdale, B. Lunn,
Hardwick Publications 1986 and 1988.

The Air War over Gwynedd, Snowdonia Aviation Historical Group
Dark Peak Wrecks, Ron Collier and Ron Wilkinson, 1979
Dark Peak Wrecks 2, Ron Collier and Ron Wilkinson, 1980
No Landing Place, Edward Doylerush, Midland Counties, 1985
Two Star Red, Gwen Moffatt 1964
Warplane Wrecks of South Wales and the Marches, Peter Durham
and Dewi Jones

Other useful material:
Action Stations, Potted histories of Britain's military airfields
and an index. Each volume covers a separate geographical area
and the series is essential for providing background
information to many of the high ground crashes.

*The Lakeland Peaks, The Peak and Pennines, The Scottish Peaks,
The Welsh Peaks,* W. A. Poucher, Constable Limited
Full of magnificent photographs and detailed routes to virtually
every significant mountain in each area. There is also useful
advice of mountain walking and essential equipment at the
beginning of each volume.

Wainwright's Lake District Guides, too numerous to list here,
are strongly recommended.

Aviation and Military Books by Post

We stock many thousands of books from all over the world for world-wide mail order.

Our quick turn-round and superb packing is unrivalled.
Free informative and illustrated catalogue on request - write or 'phone —

Midland Counties Publications
24 The Hollow, Earl Shilton,
Leicester, LE9 7NA.
Telephone: 0455 - 47091

Abbreviations

AACU	Anti-Aircraft Co-operation Unit
ADG	Air Depot Group
AFS	Advanced Flying School
AFTS	Advanced Flying Training School
AGS	Air Gunners School
AN&BS	Air Navigation & Bombing School
ANS	Air Navigation School
AONS	Air Observers' Navigation School
AOS	Air Observer School
APC	Armament Practice Camp
ATA	Air Transport Auxiliary
ATFERO	Atlantic Ferry Organisation
ATG	Air Transport Group
BATF	Beam Approach Training Flight
BG	Bomb Group
BGS	Bombing & Gunnery School
BS	Bomb Squadron
BTU	Bombing Trials Unit
CANS	Civil Air Navigation School
CCCS	Coastal Command Communications Squadron
CPF	Coastal Patrol Flight
EANS	Empire Air Navigation School
EFTS	Elementary Flying Training School
E&RFTS	Elementary & Reserve Flying Training School
FAA	Fleet Air Arm
FAF	French Air Force
FG	Fighter Group
FIS	Flying Instructors' School
FLR	First Line Reserve
FPP	Ferry Pilots' Pool
FS	Fighter Squadron
FTG	Fighter Training Group
FTS	Flying Training School
FTU	Ferry Training Unit
FU	Ferry Unit
FYS	Ferrying Squadron
HCU	(Heavy) Conversion Unit
HQSFP	Headquarters Service Ferry Pool
IAC	Irish Air Corps
ITS	Initial Training School
KG	Kampfgruppe
MCCF	Maintenance Command Communications Flight
MSFU	Merchant Ship Fighter Unit
MU	Maintenance Unit
OADF	Overseas Aircraft Delivery Flight
OAFU	(Observers) Advanced Flying Unit
OAPU	Overseas Aircraft Preparation Unit
OCU	Operational Conversion Unit
OTU	Operational Training Unit
PAFU	(Pilots) Advanced Flying Unit
RBAF	Royal Belgian Air Force
RCAF	Royal Canadian Air Force
RCN	Royal Canadian Navy
RFS	Reserve Flying School
RRE	Royal Radar Establishment
RS	Radio School
RU(A)	Repair Unit (Advanced)
SAC	School of Army Co-operation
SAN	School of Air Navigation
SFTS	Service Flying Training School
SGR	School of General Reconnaissance
SPTU	Staff Pilots' Training Unit
TCG	Troop Carrier Group
TCU	(Transport) Conversion Unit
TEU	Tactical Exercise Unit
TFPP	Training Ferry Pilots' Pool
TFW	Tactical Fighter Wing
TRS	Tactical Reconnaissance Squadron
TRW	Tactical Reconnaissance Wing
TTCF	Technical Training Command Communications Flight
TTU	Torpedo Training Unit
TWU	Tactical Weapons Unit
USAAF	United Statest Army Air Force
USN	United States Navy